Once Upon the Orient Wave

Once Upon the Orient Wave

Milton and the Arab-Muslim World

EID ABDALLAH DAHIYAT

Published by Hesperus Press Limited

28 Mortimer Street, London, W1W 7RD

www.hesperuspress.com

This book first published by Hesperus Press Limited, 2012

© Eid Abdallah Dahiyat, 2012

Designed and typeset by Bookcraft Ltd.

Printed in Jordan by Jordan National Press

ISBN: 978-1-84391-361-0

Contents

Are not all men fortified by the remembrance of the bravery, the purity, the temperance, the toil, the independence and the angelic devotion of this man, who, in a revolutionary age, taking counsel only of himself, endeavored, in his writings and in his life, to carry out the life of man to new heights of spiritual grace and dignity, without any abatement of its strength?

Ralph Waldo Emerson, 'Milton' (1838)

Preface

Studying Milton is both a challenge and a reward. It is challenging to unravel the web of Milton's intricate theological world, and his elaborate patterns of thought and frame of reference. For an Arab and a Muslim, this task is complicated further by significant differences in culture, beliefs, and approach to 'Man's first disobedience' and its subsequent consequences. Two different worlds (Milton's, and that of Arab-Islamic culture) are brought to bear on each other; the very endeavour becomes more rewarding than expected, partly through an appreciation of Milton's approach to human and divine issues, but also through the discovery of similarities connecting two disparate worlds. The scarcity of material, particularly the lack of documentary evidence, did not lessen the profound sense of satisfaction I felt throughout the course of researching and writing this book. The satisfaction I felt was mainly derived from living with excellence and with the sublime, where the mighty power of Milton's poetry and art are 'proved on my pulses'.

Now, I know that Milton is indeed the poet who lives with us for a lifetime, and, as Goethe rightly says, 'the more one grows old, the more one prizes natural gifts'. Indeed, Milton's poetry and divine fervour have the capacity of enlarging human imagination, and his lofty style puts us in touch with the beautiful and the divine. Likewise, his unswerving devotion to the cause of freedom and his liberal Christianity (unstifled by excessive theological trappings) can be appreciated by anyone, regardless of race or creed. We can all be fortified in times of personal trials and tribulations by that man's independence of mind, his magnanimity, his steadfastness in the face of adversity, and his incessant pursuit of what he believed to be 'the truth'. The firm belief of the author of *Paradise Lost* and *Samson Agonistes* in the absolute justice of heavenly judgment makes us, deluded mortals, transcend this earth and reach the heights from which we originally came. Because of these attributes, the challenge of studying John Milton has become its own reward.

The introductory chapter offers indispensable background material which places Milton's attitude to Islam in a specific historical, religious, and cultural context. The second chapter aims at determining whether Milton knew Arabic and whether he read works about Arabs and Muslims in any of the languages he knew. This study demonstrates, in the light of existing evidence, that he never studied Arabic, but that he apparently read some works, such as Leo Africanus', about certain events in Islamic history. The third chapter identifies and discusses references to Arabia and Ottoman Turkey in Milton's works, while the fourth chapter illuminates an under-explored area in Milton research: the work done by Arabic authors on the poet. The claim that he was influenced by Al-Ma'arrī is shown to lack scholarly evidence. The cult of Satan, a product of English Romanticism, had determined, to a great extent, the way the devil in *Paradise Lost* was viewed by Arab writers. Specific works in Arabic, showing this understanding, are highlighted and analysed and translations into Arabic of works by Milton are surveyed and critically examined.

An earlier version of this book was published in 1987, and was favourably received by critics and students. Unfortunately it has been out of print for some time, and

I have felt the need for a revised version. No scholar can claim an exhaustive treatment of any subject; although this is an objective that scholars and critics always try to achieve, in research, as in economics, the law of diminishing returns is sometimes at work. I initially felt that my study of John Milton and the Arab-Islamic culture reached a stage at which further additions led only to a very negligible contribution. However, I found, with the lapse of time, that more needs to be said on Milton's views of the Ottoman Turks. I have also added a postscript at the end of the final chapter on 'Milton in Arabic', in which I try to address the question that had been raised by many readers of this book: what was it in the Arab world that brought about such a great interest in Milton's writings?

Finally, I should sincerely like to express my utmost gratitude and heartfelt thanks to my lifelong friend Professor Muhammad Yusif Shaheen for his encouragement and much-needed advice.

I

The West Learns of Islam and Arabic

The English attitude to Islam in the Middle Ages and during the Renaissance is a wide and far-reaching subject, inseparable from the attitude of European Christendom as a whole. But my aim is limited to establishing a series of facts that help place Milton in a particular religious, historical, and cultural context, in the light of which his knowledge of and attitude to Islam (as well as any influence Islamic learning[1] might have exercised on him) can be assessed.

Europe received most of its information about Arabs and Muslims by way of Syria (conquered in AD 634), of Spain (held 711–1492), and of Sicily (held 825–1091). The ideas about Islam formulated in the Christian east, particularly by the Greek-speaking Syrians and some Christian Arabs, had an enduring influence throughout the west. St John of Damascus (d.749), who knew Arabic, Greek, and Syriac, was the author of two dialogues which have been described as 'an effective apology for Christianity and a manual for the guidance of Christians in their arguments with Moslems'.[2] In his *Chronographia*, the Byzantine Theophanes the Confessor (c.758–818) followed St John. This Syro-Byzantine source of information was strengthened further by the Arabic *Risāla*, usually attributed to Abd-al-Masīḥ ibn Isḥāq al-Kindī. Al-Kindī, apparently a Nestorian priest, wrote his treatise, a bitter attack on prophet Muḥammad and Islamic tenets, as an answer to a letter sent to him by the Muslim Abdullah ibn

Isma'īl al-Hāshimī, who tried to convert Al-Kindī to Islam. It covers almost all the traditional arguments of Christian polemic writers against Islam, and was translated by Peter of Toledo (late twelfth century) for inclusion in the Cluniac Corpus. The polemic war against Islam had begun.

During the era of the Crusades (twelfth and thirteenth centuries), European hostility to Islam reached a tragic climax. The Crusading oral and written literature helped fix certain stereotypes and strengthen the Syro-Byzantine polemic image of Islam. The rise of the Ottoman Turks as a major Muslim power aggravated European fears and animosity. Beginning in the mid-fourteenth century, the Turkish victories culminated in the acquisition of Constantinople (1453) and of the whole of the Balkan Peninsula. Having failed to conquer Islam by sheer military force or by missionary work, Europe succeeded in establishing a deformed image of Islam, its teachings, and its prophet in European consciousness.

Continually augmented and fervently fostered by Christian missionaries, these polemic stereotypes and misrepresentations became so dogmatic that by the time Milton was writing they already enjoyed the status of established religious authority. They still determine, to a great extent, the way Islam and its followers are viewed in the west, as Edward Said has shown so cogently.

Paradoxically, while Europe was conducting a campaign of endless polemic against Islam, it was steadily absorbing the great heritage of Islamic culture and learning. With original contributions and innovative discoveries of their own, the Arabs transmitted to Europe a rich legacy of Hellenistic, Persian, and Indian learning and knowledge. Without the fruits of Islamic civilisation, Europe would never have achieved the progress it enjoyed in the Renaissance and still enjoys. Spain and Sicily were the centres of Islamic influence on Western Europe; the Palermo court of Roger II (r.1130–54) and of Frederick II (r.1296–1337) looked more Islamic than Christian. Interestingly, Roger II, who spoke and read Arabic, was the patron of the celebrated Muslim geographer and cartographer Al-Idrīsi (d.1166). When Frederick II was excommunicated by Pope Gregory IX in 1239, he was charged, among other things, with 'displays of friendliness towards Islam'. Muslim Spain (Andalusia) played the most crucial role in the revival of learning in medieval Europe. The Mozarabes, the Christians of Spain who became half-Arabicised, helped in the transmission of Islamic learning to the Europeans of the north. In Cordoba, Seville, Granada, and Toledo, schools flourished and translation throve. Toledo (captured from the Arabs in 1085) remained a centre of Islamic learning under Christian rule. It was even chosen (in 1250) by the Order of Preachers as the site for their School of Oriental Studies, designed to prepare missionaries to Muslims and Jews.

The first English scholar to travel to study at the Arab schools in Spain was one of King Alfred's early lecturers at Oxford, John Scotus (or John Erigena, c.810–77). He is believed to have studied Arabic and Chaldean. Writing in the eighteenth century, Thomas Warton (1728–90) praised the role Arab schools in Spain played in the introduction of learning to England. He pointed out that, at the beginning of the eleventh century, many Englishmen from the clergy and the laity attended those schools, establishing a trend which continued for a long time. Daniel Merlac (or Morley, d.1190), astronomer and mathematician, studied at Toledo's famous school and returned to England with a

valuable collection of books. In his own works, he quotes
frequently from Arabic and Greek philosophers, and
praises the superiority of the former. Adelard of Bath,
who probably learned Arabic in Sicily or the Holy Land,
is credited with producing a dozen or more original works
or translations from the Arabic on philosophical, math-
ematical, and astronomical subjects, as well as a treatise on
falconry, the earliest book of its kind known in Western
Europe. Early in the thirteenth century Michael Scot,
who studied at Toledo, translated Aristotle's treatises on
animals from Arabic, and became the astrologer at the
court of the emperor Frederick II.

Robert of Ketton (also called Robertus Retenesis, Robert
of Chester and Robert of Reading) was by far the most
important English Arabist of the Middle Ages. He was
working in Barcelona in 1136, under the great Italian scholar
and translator from the Arabic, Plato of Tivoli, and he also
befriended Hermann the Dalmatian, apparently for the
purpose of studying astronomy. As a result of his interest in
astronomy and geometry, he compiled a set of astronomical
tables based on those of Al-Battāni and Al-Zarāqāli, and
revised the tables of Al-Khawārizmi. He also translated the
algebra of Al-Khawārizmi (in 1145), marking the beginning
of European algebra. (The word 'algorithm' is derived from
Al-Khawārizmi.)

However, Robert of Ketton's greatest achievement was
his translation of the Qur'ān (the first in Europe) from
Arabic into Latin. Done at the instance of Peter the
Venerable, abbot of Cluny, that translation, with a preface
and marginal annotations attributed to Peter of Poitiers,
was completed between 6 July and 31 December 1143.
Supplementary to it, Peter the Venerable wrote a *Treatise*

Against Mohammedanism. Unfortunately, the translated text abounds in gross inaccuracies which betray Ketton's ignorance of the rhetorical subtleties and profound eloquence of the Arabic of the Qur'ān. Moreover, Ketton 'was always liable to heighten or exaggerate a harmless text in order to give it a nasty or licentious ring, or to prefer an improbable but unpleasant interpretation of the meaning to a likely but normal and decent one'.[3] The result was not the Qur'ān, but rather a mutilated rendering of it, larded with explanatory annotations having no basis in historical fact or religious meaning. Indeed, in his preface Ketton says that he experienced 'considerable difficulty' in the translation.

In parenthesis at this point, it is worth saying that, for many people, as a supreme work of art the Qur'ān is untranslatable. It must be read in Arabic. Commenting on his own translation of the Qur'ān, Muhammad Marmaduke Pickthall (1875–1936) says that the aim of his work is:

> [T]o present to English readers what Muslims the world over hold to be the meaning of the words of the Qur'ān and the nature of the book, in not unworthy language and concisely, with a view to the requirements of English Muslims. It may be reasonably claimed that no Holy Scripture can be fairly presented by one who disbelieves its inspiration and its message; and this is the first English translation of the Qur'ān by an Englishman who is a Muslim. Some of the translations include commentations offensive to Muslims. And almost all employ a style of language which Muslims at once recognize as unworthy. The Qur'ān cannot be translated. This is the belief of traditional Sheykhs and the view of the present writer. The book is here

rendered almost literally and every effort has been made to choose befitting language. But the result is not the Glorious Qur'ān, that inimitable symphony, the very sounds of which move men to tears and ecstasy. It is only an attempt to present the meaning of the Qur'ān – and peradventure something of the charm in English. It can never take the place of the Qur'ān in Arabic, nor is it meant to do so.[4]

In spite of its defects, Robert of Ketton's annotated translation enjoyed a considerable circulation in manuscript, and provided new material for fresh attacks against Islam. The gulf between the historical Islam on the one hand and its polemic representations on the other had been widened.

Ketton's translation was first printed in Basel in 1543, with a preface by Martin Luther himself, and was reissued with a preface by Philip Melanchthon in 1550.

At the time, knowledge of Arabic was viewed as a vehicle for spiritual crusades against Muslims. This trend was encouraged by missionaries and remained a cornerstone of Arabic and Islamic studies in the west for centuries to come. Acting upon the recommendations of the Spanish Raymond Lull (c.1235–1315), the greatest missionary of medieval Europe, the Church Council of Vienna (1311) decided to establish chairs in Greek and oriental languages (especially Arabic, Hebrew, and Syriac) at Paris, Oxford, Bologna, Avignon, and Salamanca. But missionary hopes for the conversion of Muslims were doomed to failure. On the contrary: under the banner of the Ottoman Empire, Muslims were on the march, knocking at the doors of Vienna itself.

The English Franciscan friar Roger Bacon (1214–94) was the only person at the time to propose that languages, including Arabic, should be studied 'for reasons other than missionary purposes':

> His first reason for the study of Hebrew, Greek, and Arabic is '*propter studium sapientiae absolutum*' which includes the knowledge necessary to carry out the rites of the church. His second reason is for the better maintenance of commercial, judicial, and international relations. Thirdly, he wishes linguistic studies to aid in the conversion of the infidel, and fourthly, to reprove those incapable of conversion. He feels that it is not only harmful, 'but very embarrassing when among all the learned men of the Latins, prelates and princes do not find a single one who knows how to interpret a letter of Arabic or Greek nor to reply to a message as is sometimes the case. For example, I learned that the Soldanus of Babylon [Egypt] wrote to my lord, the present king of France, and there was not found in the whole learned body in Paris nor in the whole kingdom of France a man who knew how satisfactorily to explain a letter nor to make the necessary reply to the message.' Bacon admitted that he himself did not write Arabic, but only Hebrew, Greek, and Latin.[5]

Meanwhile, English chroniclers, travellers, and literary men were bequeathing the missionary image of Islam to posterity. In 1217 Matthew Paris (1195–1259) became a monk at St Albans Abbey, which at that time was a place of art and learning and where the writing of history was especially encouraged.

In writing of the year 622 (the year of the Muslims' Hijra to Medīna), Paris assembled many absurd and fabulous details about Islam, which were current in his own time. Similarly, Ranulf Higden (d.1364) was no better a historian as far as Islam was concerned. Higden was a Benedictine monk at the monastery of St Warburg at Chester. His fame rests on *Polychronicon*, a Latin history of the world to 1342. It was the most comprehensive history to have then appeared, and was popular for the next two centuries.[6] The English version by John Trevisa appeared in 1387, and was subsequently printed by Caxton in 1482, by Wynkyn de Worde in 1495, and by Peter Treveris in 1527. Although reasonably accurate on the subjects of Muslim fasting at Ramadān, and the pilgrimage to Mecca, Higden's book falls within the medieval crusading framework.

These accounts of historians, coupled with those of travellers, contributed to the circulation of more distorted and purely imaginative material about Islam. A book entitled *The Travels of John Mandeville* is a case in point. Relating the travels of a legendary figure who was said to have left England for Jerusalem in 1322, the book contained erroneous and offensive material regarding Islamic doctrines and the life of Prophet Muḥammad. Originally written in French, it remained a basic reference in eleven European languages (including English) for more than five centuries.

The story of the Prophet's coffin may serve as an example of how those chroniclers and writers of travel literature resorted to sheer imagination to supply information on historical Islamic events. According to European accounts, the Prophet's coffin was suspended in air by means of huge lodestones fixed in the roof of the Grand Mosque at Mecca. Although this legend does not appear in English literature until the Renaissance, it was well known during the Middle Ages. Brother Felix Fabri, who visited Palestine in 1481–3, relayed it.[7] Interestingly, John Milton uses this legend in *Eikonoklastes*: 'We meet next with a comparison, how apt let them judge who have traveled to Mecca, that the Parliament has hung the majestie of kingship in an airy imagination of regality between the Privilege of both Houses, like the Tomb of Mahomet.'[8]

Along with their European counterparts, English lyricists, romance writers, and playwrights used the available information about Islam and Muslims to create patterns of references and allusions, images and echoes, which were destined to remain strongly entrenched in the European literary imagination to the present day. Any casual reader of medieval literary works, especially romances, can spot a myriad of defamatory references, and easily detect the spirit of the Crusades lurking in the background.

Travel literature of the sixteenth and seventeenth centuries helped circulate similar material on a wider scale. George Sandys, despite the fact he had positive words to say about Islam's emphasis on good deeds, attacks the Prophet Muhammad bitterly.[9] Sandys and other travellers did not differ much from their medieval predecessors. Norman Daniel aptly sums up the case as follows:

> Travellers always seem to show independent judgment most when they are speaking of actual encounters, and least when they discuss theory, dogma, or the life of Muhammad. They easily confused what they saw, what they were told, and what they had long ago read in books... Most travellers of the seventeenth century added practical observations of their own, but based their accounts of Islam as a religion not on their own direct experience, but on tradition inherited from the

medieval West. ... Many travellers genuinely sought
to correct misapprehensions; yet even when their
approach was academic... the general outline of the
image of Islam remained the same.[10]

The romances of *The Sowdone of Babylone* and *Guy of
Warwick* deal with Christian knight errantry all over
the Muslim world. In the romance of *Bevis of Hampton*,
numerous episodes are assembled to make up the story
of Bevis' love for the daughter of a 'Saracen' king named
Ermin. Bevis' adventures centre on his efforts to maintain
his reputation as a Christian knight against what is called
'pagan treachery'. The celebrated romance of Floris and
Blancheflour is dismissive of Muslims, referring to them
as 'Saracens' and 'infidels'. It has to be said that Muslims
in the Middle Ages also thought of Europeans as uncul-
tured and barbarous. Usamah ibn Munqidh (d.1188), who
had contacts with the Crusaders, had little or no respect for
them. Ibn Khaldun (1332–1406) held similar opinions.[11]

However, despite the hostile attitude these sources
exhibit, there were also references of respect and admiration
for the achievements of learned Muslim men. The 'Man
of Physick' in Chaucer's prologue to *The Canterbury Tales*
knew, among others, Muslim physicians such as 'Raziz,
Avycen, Averrois, Damascien'. Also, Chaucer's 'A treatise
on the Astrolabe' is partly translation and partly adaptation
from Messahala's *Compositio et operatio Astrolabii*, a Latin
rendering of an eighth century Arabian work. Chaucer's
version has been praised as the first work written in English
upon a scientific instrument.

The irony in all this is that medieval English literature,
as part of the European literary heritage, owed much to the

literary forms developed by Arab writers. Donald Sands has pointed out that many romances, despite their anti-Muslim sentiment, 'derive by devious and now obscure means from Arabic tales. No one has really assessed the debt western European narrative art of the medieval period owes to the genius of the Arab world, but in many romances its influence must be great, although so distant that perhaps no one now will ever be able to indicate its nature exactly and accurately.'[12] In European lyric poetry, the indebtedness is even more striking.

The subject of the relationship in Muslim Spain between Arabic poetry and the troubadours (who transmitted it to various European countries) is still inadequately researched and tenuously understood but there is a consensus among scholars that certain Arabic literary forms and themes, particularly those developed in Muslim Spain, did infiltrate into medieval European literature.

The origins of the medieval baroque picaresque narrative can be sought in Arabic writing. In the eighth century, Abdullah ibn al-Muqafa translated a series of animal fables of Indian origin into Arabic. Known as the book of *Kalila wa Dimna*, the fables were translated into Spanish for Alfonso the Wise (1252–84). John of Capua, a converted Jew, made a Latin translation from a Hebrew version produced by a certain Rabbi Joel in the early part of the thirteenth century. He called this Latin version the *Directorium Vitae Humanae* and it achieved wider popularity than the Alfonsive work and was translated into most European languages, including a Spanish rendering at Zaragoza in 1493.[13] In 1552, it was translated into Italian by Anton Francesco Doni, and Thomas North's *Moral Philosophy of Doni* (1570) was the first of many English versions. The Latin and vernacular

versions were used for many decades by writers and drama-
tists, including for example, by Massinger in the third act
of *The Guardian*. Likewise, the Arabic *Book of Sindbād* (not
the famous Arabian Nights story) was translated from a
Sanskrit original into Hebrew as *Sindabār*. The Hebrew
version was probably derived from the thirteenth century
Spanish work known as *Libro de los Enqannos*, and a Latin
version, *Historia Septem Sapientium,* which was the source
of many verse romances, such as the English *Seven Sages of
Rome*.

The greatest influence on the development of the
European picaresque narrative was that of the Arabic
maqāmāt. Maqāmāt (sq. *maqāmah*) are conversational pieces
that tell of the adventures and escapades of a vagabond
hero. In order to earn his living, the hero, who is endowed
with a powerful literary skill, engages in numerous tricks
and escapades. Badī az-Zamān al-Hamadhānī (969–1007)
wrote *maqāmāt* in *saj* (rhymed prose) – usually inter-
spersed with verses – where Isa ibn Hishām figures as the
hero. Al-Harīrī (d.1122) changed the names of his fictional
characters to Al-Harith ibn Hammām (the narrator) and
Abū Zayd of Sarūj (the wandering hero). Al-Harīrī is
the better artist, however. His manipulation of dialogues,
which create dramatic contexts within which the action
is developed, attests to superb artistic craftsmanship. The
episodic structure of the *maqāmah* is made coherent by the
dramatic vitality and vividness of the story. The Spanish
Jewish author al-Harīzī translated al-Harīrī's *maqāmāt* from
Arabic into Hebrew. He even composed his own *maqāmāt*
which he called *Tahkemoni* with a hero named Hebre the
Kenite (taken from 2 Samuel 23:8). Two Spanish scholars,
Menedez y Pelayo and González Palencia, have identified

the affinity of the *maqāmāt* of Arabic baroque picaresque narrative with the picaro literature. The picaresque element also figures prominently in what are called *zajal* poems. Written in ironic colloquial Arabic, these poems vividly depict a low life of taverns and marketplaces. Ibn Quzmān (d.1160) in particular portrays a life characterised by great permissiveness and moral laxity, led mostly by the twelfth century aristocratic class in Muslim Spain. The *zajal* poems became popular and ultimately found their way into purely romance poetry such as the popular form from the Iberian Peninsula, known as the *villancico*.

Although the relationship between Arabic love poetry on the one hand and the Provencal troubadour lyrics on the other needs more careful investigation; comparisons of themes, images, metrical forms, sentiments, and concepts in both are very fruitful. Gustave von Grunebaum's research has shown to what extent the Christian poets 'duplicated, or adopted from, patterns prepared by their Muslim confreres. Even if every other coincidence of mood, of theme, of approach, could be denied or explained away, the parallels in poetic technique would suffice to establish a considerable degree of troubadour dependency on Arabic models.'[14]

Without going into details, my aim in this book is to show that the kind of love expressed in the *muwashshaḥāt*, in the odes (*qasidās*) of Ibn Zaydūn, and in Ibn Ḥazm's *The Dove's Necklace* was not without impact on Provencal poetry, and, consequently, on European lyric poetry.

The *muwashshaḥāt* were developed at the courts of the Arab princes of Spain by cultivated poets in the late ninth or early tenth century. The origin, development, and poetics of the *muwashshaḥāt* are explained by Ibn Khaldūn (1332–1406) as follows: 'The *muwashshaḥāt* consist of "branches" [*ghusūn*] and "strings" [*simt*] in great number and different metres. A certain number [of "branches" and "strings"] is called a single verse [stanza]. There must be the same number of rhymes in the "branches" [of each stanza] and the same metre [for the "branches" of the whole poem] throughout the whole poem. The largest number of stanzas employed is seven. Each stanza contains as many "branches" as is consistent with purpose and method. Like the *qasīda*, the *muwashshahā* is used for erotic and laudatory poetry.'

These strophic poems were probably first invented by the blind poet Mugaddam ibn Mu'āfā al-Qabrī at the court of the Emir Abdullah (r.888–912) They were, to a great extent, an Andalusian version of some poetic versions developed in the Arab East by poets such as Abu Nuwās (dc.803) to ridicule and ironise certain outmoded love conventions of Arabic poetry. Ibn Bassam (d.1147) notes that 'the *muwashshahāt* are metres which the people of al-Andalus use abundantly in the composition of *ghazel* [erotic] and *nasīb* [laudatory] poems, such that on hearing them there are torn open the collars – nay even the hearts – of gently-nurtured ladies.' Though not a poet of *muwashshahāt*, Ibn Zaydūn (1003–71), one of the most outstanding of the Arab poets of Spain, expressed similar sentiments. An Umayyad princess named Wallādah was Ibn Zaydūn's beloved and inspirer. The love ideals and sentiments exhibited in the *muwashshahāt* and in the odes of Ibn Zaydūn were immortalised by Ibn Ḥazm.

Ibn Ḥazm's life (993–1064) is divided into two parts. The first was spent at the courts of Umayyad princes, while the second was devoted to studies and writing on various subjects (mainly religious). His celebrated little book *Tawq al-Hammāma fil Ulfa was ullāf* (*The Dove's Necklace, on Love and Lovers*) was written during the first period. That booklet, which presents the refined but permissive attitudes of Cordoba's upper class, is considered an important document embodying the doctrine of courtly love two centuries before the poets of Provence.

All the paraphernalia of courtly love are here. The similarities are striking and precise. As in courtly love poetry, an assumed name to conceal the lady's identity is used. There are also the familiar references to the problems caused by the guards, husbands, and slanderers. There is the idea that love, considered as a noble emotion rooted in the human soul, requires secrecy. Since the delight of the lover is always in the presence of his beloved, separation is viewed as the cause of suffering and all the ills that beset lovers. Submission of the lover is indicative of his faithful love. Though not denying the physical, Ibn Ḥazm stresses the joys of spiritual love. There are also the exaggerated descriptions of the physical beauty of women.

While it might have been natural to expect the transfer of poetic forms and sentiments from Muslim Spain to Provence and ultimately to other parts of Europe, there are some specific examples which show how the transmission process worked.

The crusading journey to the East (1101–2) of the first Aquitanian minnesinger [troubadour], Count Guillaume IX de Poitiers (1071–1127), obviously resulted in a complete change in the spirit and technique of his poetry. After his return from the Holy Land, the rhythm and the general structure of his songs suddenly become strongly reminiscent of the *muwashshaḥāt*. Macabru (dc.1185) and Pierre d'Auvergne (dc.1180), two other exponents of the new style, went to Spain and proved receptive to Andalusian influences.

There was also oral transmission as a result of long and permanent contact between Muslims and Christians. Bilingualism in Spain was common, and eight or more centuries of such intimate contact would have fostered cultural interaction and continuity. Translations from Arab poetry and prose in Muslim Spain were also available, as Petrus Alphonsi described in 1106. Eleanor of Aquitaine, the granddaughter of one of the first French troubadours, married Prince Henry of England after she was divorced by Prince Louis of France. By his marriage to her, Henry, who had already inherited Normandy and Anjou (1150–1), gained control of Aquitaine. Eleanor became very popular in England, especially in literary circles. Thomas of Britain's *Tristram and Ysolt* was written for her and Wace's *Brut* was also dedicated to her. Although there is no conclusive evidence that the famous troubadour poet Bernard de Vantadour went with her to England, one poem of Vantadour's seems to indicate that he may have crossed the Channel.[15] The link between Provence and England was perpetuated by Eleanor of Provence (d.1291), who married Henry III. Both the father and mother of Eleanor figure among the Provencal poets, and she is said to have composed an heroic poem in her native language while still a child. Thus, from the middle of the twelfth century (roughly the golden age of the troubadours), England had almost unbroken contact with the French troubadours. Studies of the medieval and Renaissance English lyric have amply demonstrated the indebtedness of this genre to Platonic, Ovidian, and Petrarchan love conventions.

The influence of Arabic love tradition has often been neglected by scholars. In fact, there is lamentable unwillingness to acknowledge the influence of Islamic heritage on various aspects of Western civilisation. M.M. Watt has written: 'For our indebtedness to Islam, we Europeans have a blind spot. We sometimes belittle the extent and importance of Islamic influence in our heritage, and sometimes overlook it altogether ... To try to cover it, and deny it, is a mark of false pride.'[16] If the topic is investigated more thoroughly, the influence of Arabic literary heritage on European lyrical poetry and narrative art may prove to be enormous, far-reaching, and pervasive.

Of special significance in this respect, at least as far as Milton is concerned, is the alleged indebtedness of Dante to Arabic literary heritage. There are several studies of Islamic influences on Dante's *Divine Comedy*.[17] Miguel Asin, using scholarship of unmatched excellence and a far-reaching knowledge of Islam and its heritage, prints the Arabic text with its parallels in the *Comedy*. He shows that Dante drew on different versions based on the story of Prophet Muhammad's ascension (Mi'raj) to heaven. Parallel passages from Dante's *Divine Comedy* and from his Arabian sources are given and a wealth of detail is used to strengthen and support the overall thesis. Nevertheless, Asin achieved all this only on comparative data. He did not come up with any documented evidence of the translation of any of those Mi'raj stories into any European language or of Dante's familiarity with any possible translation.

Other scholars have shown that a lengthy and detailed account of the Prophet's journey through heaven under the guidance of the archangel Gabriel was translated in the third quarter of the thirteenth century for Alfonso X of Spain, showing that the subject, treated on a popular level, was accessible to readers of Spanish as well as of Latin and French, with copies in those languages having been preserved. Moreover, it has been possible to show that Italians were among those acquainted with the work in translation and that the text and related materials were indeed widely known throughout Western Europe. There can be no doubt that Dante could have read it. Franz Rosenthal wrote, 'If we had documentary evidence to the effect that Dante did read a work on the *Mi'raj* in translation and not merely that he *might* have read it, this greatest single instance of Muslim influence upon Western Literature would advance from possibility to probability, and, perhaps, even certainty.'

Another commentator, R.A. Nicolson, finds similarities between the works of Dante and those of the famous Muslim mystic Ibnu'l 'Arabi:

> Ibnu'l 'Arabi's descriptions of Hell, Paradise, and the Beatific vision are reproduced by Dante with a closeness that can scarcely be fortuitous. The infernal regions, the astronomical heavens, the circles of the mystic rose, the choirs of angels around the focus of divine light, the three circles symbolizing the Trinity all are described by Dante exactly as Ibnu'l 'Arabi described them. Dante tells how, as he mounted higher and higher in Paradise, his love was made stronger and his spiritual vision more intense by seeing Beatrice grow more and more beautiful. The same idea occurs in a poem of Ibnu'l 'Arabi written about a century earlier ... It may be added that Ibnu'l 'Arabi too had a Beatrice, Nizam, the beautiful and accomplished daughter of Makinu'ddin – and that owing to the scandal caused by the mystical odes which he composed in her honour he wrote a commentary on them in order to convince his critics that they were

wrong. Similarly in the 'Convito' Dante declares his intention to interpret the esoteric meaning of fourteen love-songs which he had composed at an earlier date, and the subject of which had led to the erroneous belief that they dealt with sensual rather than intellectual love. In short, the parallelism, both general and particular, reaches so far that only one conclusion is possible … The *Mi'raj* or Ascension of the prophet together with popular and philosophical conceptions of the after-life – derived from Muslim traditionists and such writers as Fārabi, Avicenna, Ghazālī, and Ibnu'l 'Arabi – must have passed into the common stock of literary culture that was accessible to the best minds in Europe in the thirteenth century.[18]

The above merely hints at what is still to be discovered by scholars of medieval and Renaissance literature who become familiar with Arabic literature.

The advent of the Renaissance added a new humanistic interest in the Arabic language to the previous motive of missionary zeal. The revival of Arabic studies in Europe is usually associated with Italian, Spanish, and French scholars, driven by a variety of political, religious, commercial, and linguistic motives. In 1536 the French humanist Guillaume Postal was sent by King Francis I to Egypt and Turkey to collect manuscripts. After his return to France, he was appointed professor of Greek, Hebrew, and Arabic at the newly founded College de France. The Maronite scholar Gabriel Sionita (1577–1648) joined the Maronite college in Rome (established in 1548), and then went to Paris where he became professor of Arabic. Matthias Pastor (1599–1658), a German scholar from Heidelberg, learnt

Arabic from Sionita in the winter of 1624–5. In 1626 Pastor was appointed Hebrew lecturer in New College, Oxford, where he also lectured in Arabic and Syriac. One of his students was Edward Pococke, the greatest English Arabist of the Renaissance.

In Spain, the famous humanist Juan Luis Vives (1492–1540), who was a friend of Erasmus and tutor of Princess Mary of England, strongly supported the study of Arabic for purely missionary purposes. Among the prominent Italian humanists of the early Renaissance were Giorgio Valla (1447–1500) and Giovanni Pico della Mirandola (1463–1494). The latter acquired many Arabic manuscripts, and in 1498 his library had seven books in Arabic. The catalogue of the Vatican library in 1481 shows a total of twenty-two codices in Arabic. In 1638, when Milton visited that library, it must have had more Arabic books.

Among the other Italian humanists who were involved in Arabic studies were Teseo Ambrogio and Agostino Giustiniani. Ambrogio (1469–1540) was the author of the famous *Introductio in Chaldaicam linguam, Syriacam atque Armeniam, et decem, alias linguas, characterum differentium alphabeta circiter quadraginta ta, et eorumdem invicem conformatio* (Pavia, 1539), which includes a section de *Arabis, Punicisque consonantibus*, with an Arabic translation of a part of the third chapter of the gospel of Luke. This work proved a very valuable philological tool for other orientalists. According to Karl Dannenfeldt:

> Another Italian humanist who contributed greatly to the expansion of Arabic studies was Agostino Giustiniani (1479–1536). This bishop of Nebbia in Corsica, well-versed in Latin, Greek, Hebrew,

Chaldean and Arabic, was known as a great collector of Greek and oriental manuscripts. In 1516 Pietro Porro published for him in Genoa two thousand copies of a polyglot Psalter, the justly celebrated *Psalterium Nebiense*. This work gave excellent service to those interested in oriental languages, for it presented the psalms in parallel columns in Hebrew, Chaldean, Greek, Arabic, and in three Latin versions... Numerous other Italian humanists acquired some knowledge of Arabic. Johannes Annius Viterbiensis (ca.1432–1502), the editor of the collection of forgeries known as the *Antiquitatum variarum volumina* XVIII, knew Arabic, as did Alexius Pedemontanus (d.1550). Hieronymous Aleander (1480–1542), the Italian scholar who opposed Luther at the Diet of Worms, diligently applied himself to the study of Arabic, Chaldean, and Hebrew before he was twenty-four years old.[19]

In Protestant Europe the influence of Islamic culture was overwhelming. W. Wilson Cash, who served for many years as the secretary of the Church Missionary Society in London, wrote that Islam 'offered to a world tired of its priests and their authority a new conception of a religious democracy, where religion was a lay movement stripped of all ecclesiastical trappings … The Moslem mind stimulated Christian thinkers to a formidable criticism of the Catholic position and to intellectual attacks upon the priests, and the doctrine of the Mass, and in this way played an important part in initiating the Renaissance.'[20]

The influence of Islam on Protestantism and on the European Renaissance could also be seen as contributing to the emancipation of the human mind from intellectual shackles. The Islamic doctrine of *Ijtihad* (independent judgment in theological questions) reflects Islam's respect for human intellectual creativity. Islam also contributed to the notion of the inner light (which is really grounded in the rejection of clerical mediation between God and man).

All of this suggests that Renaissance humanists found in Islam a new invigorating spirit. For one thing, the Protestant rejection of clerical authority (expressed, among other works, in Milton's *The Reason of Church Government Urged Against Prelaty*) and belief in the individual inner light correspond to the Islamic rejection of intermediaries between the believer and God. Nicholas Rescher, identifying three major waves in the influence of Islamic philosophical thought on Europe, points out that the study of that thought 'contributed to the Protestant intellectual ferment – with various results of which one of the most striking is that in one significant instance Arabic philosophy served as a stimulus to the philosophico-religious ideology of English pietism'.[21] Protestant literalism gave an impetus to Arabic scholarship in Europe as an adjunct to the study of biblical authority. Not only was the study of Arabic crucial to the Protestant polemic war against Muslims, but, being a Semitic tongue, Arabic helps in understanding the Hebrew text of the Old Testament. Moreover, one of the versions of the text of the New Testament was in Arabic. Any serious scholarly endeavour in the field of biblical textual criticism and verification would have benefited greatly from a knowledge of the Arabic language.

One of the leading Arabists of the Renaissance, a man who did much to advance Arabic studies in Protestant Europe, was the Protestant convert Joseph Justus Scaliger (1540–1609). Scaliger was proficient in both Hebrew and

Arabic, which helped revolutionise the study of ancient chronology. But the growth and development of an important centre of Arabic studies in Protestant Europe really began with the appointment of Thomas Erpenius as professor of oriental languages at Leiden in 1613. He held the post until his death in 1624 and was succeeded by his former pupil James Golius (1596–1667). Erpenius and Golius made outstanding contributions to the development of Arabic studies by their teaching, their preparation of texts, and their assiduity in collecting manuscripts. Erpenius published Arabic versions of biblical books, and translated into Latin the history of Tirjīs al-Makīn ibn al-Amīd. The work of the Dutch scholars in its turn served as an inspiration to English scholars and patrons.

In England, most relevant to any possible contact by Milton with Islamic writings, there had been some Arabic manuscripts in the episcopal library at York early in the Middle Ages. In 1477, William Caxton printed the first English book, *The Dictes and Sayings of the Philosophers*, which was a translation by Anthony Woodville, 2nd Earl Rivers, from a French translation of the Latin *Liber philosophorum moralim* – a rendering of a collection of sayings gleaned from ancient sages and philosophers compiled in eleventh century Egypt by Al-Mubashshir ibn Fātik. Because of its instructive and didactic character Ibn Fātik's book enjoyed great popularity. The different versions (Latin, Spanish, French, and English) were widely distributed during the early years of printing and contributed much to general instructional literature, a type which, until the time of the Enlightenment, dominated the publishers' market in Europe.

The earliest English humanist who we know knew Arabic was probably Robert Wakefeld (d.1537). After his graduation from Cambridge University in 1513/14, he went abroad to study oriental languages and became professor of Hebrew at Louvain. In 1530 Wakefeld taught Hebrew at Oxford, and in 1532 he was appointed a canon in the newly founded King's College, Oxford, later Christ Church, where he wrote the first book featuring Hebrew and Arabic characters to be printed in England.

Richard Pace (c.1482–1536), a friend of Robert Wakefeld, also knew Arabic. Pace served as a diplomat and as a dean of St Paul's. He studied under Thomas Langton, bishop of Winchester, who made the young Pace his *amanuensis* and then sent him to study at Padua. From there he went to Ferrara where Erasmus, writing in 1521, speaks of having met him,[22] although there is no evidence that Erasmus knew Arabic.

Richard Argentine (d.1568), a physician and a divine, wrote *Ad Oxonienses et Cantabrigienses pro lingua Arabica beneficio principum restituenda*, a plea for the restoration of the study of Arabic at Oxford and Cambridge.[23]

Another divine who was also a skilled linguist in several eastern languages, including Chaldaic, Arabic, and Ethiopic tongues was Richard Brett (c.1560–1637). Because of his knowledge of biblical languages, Brett was appointed by James I as one of the translators of the Bible into English. Another of the thirty-two scholars chosen for the new Authorised Version of the Old Testament was Miles Smith, said to have 'Hebrew at his fingers' ends', and to whom Chaldaic, Syriac, and Arabic were almost as familiar as his native tongue.

Yet another of the King James Bible translation team was William Bedwell (c.1561–1632), who did much to advance Arabic studies in England. Bedwell called attention to the importance of Arabic as a 'tongue which was the only language of religion and the chief language of diplomacy and business from the Fortunate Islands to the China Sea'.[24] Drawn into Arabic studies through his interest in mathematics and astronomy, Bedwell had printed at the Plantin press at Antwerp a manuscript translation of the Epistles of St John into Arabic, made probably in the fourteenth century, and in his 'Preface to the Pious Reader' he sums up in a forcible manner the various arguments which may be urged on behalf of the study of the language.[25] He also imported from Leiden the first font of Arabic type to be brought to England. His greatest achievement in the field of Arabic studies was his work *The Arabian Trudgman, that is, certain Arabicke termes, as names of places, titles of honour … expounded according to their etymologie.* This famous lexicon in seven folio manuscript volumes contains an index of all the surahs of the Qur'ān, and includes Hebrew, Syriac, Chaldee, and Arabic words.

To compile his Arabic lexicon Bedwell used the Qur'ān, Arabic versions of the Bible, the works of Avicenna, and a translation of *Euclid* by Nasir-ed-Din. As a result of this work, Bedwell has a lasting place in the history of Arabic scholarship.

Bedwell's disciple in the field of Arabic studies was Edward Pococke (or Pocock), the elder (1604–91). Pococke was supervised in his early Arabic studies at Oxford by both Bedwell and by the German Arabist Matthias Pastor. After his graduation, he was appointed chaplain to the English Levant Company at Aleppo. During his time in Aleppo (1630–6) he mastered Arabic, which he read and spoke fluently, studied Hebrew, Samaritan, Syriac, and Ethiopic, and, with the help of learned Muslims and Jews, collected manuscripts. As a means of obtaining Arabic manuscripts, Pococke appointed a Syrian, al-Darwish Ahmad, as his agent and copyist. Through letters written by the Syrian to Pococke after he left Aleppo, we learn much about the trade in manuscripts at the time. The collection of Arabic manuscripts by Pococke was encouraged and commissioned by Archbishop Laud, who, in 1634, as a minister of Charles I, obtained a royal letter to the Levant Company requiring that every ship returning from the East should bring back one Persian or Arabic manuscript. Pococke returned to England in 1636, and in July of that year Laud, who, as Chancellor of Oxford University at that time, had established an Arabic chair, appointed Pococke a professor of Arabic. Pococke had already brought with him from Aleppo a copy of Meydani's collection of 6,013 Arabic proverbs and he translated it into English but did not publish it at the time.

Pococke returned again to the East in 1637 accompanied by his friend John Greaves, professor of astronomy at Oxford. He lived in Constantinople until August 1640, and Greaves left for Egypt to collect manuscripts and make some astronomical observations.

Edward Pococke was motivated by a variety of religious, commercial, and scholarly considerations. A knowledge of the Arabic language and an understanding of Islam were indeed required if English trade with that part of the world were to be profitable. But the old missionary goal was not abandoned. Pococke and his patron, Laud, were, after all, clergymen. Thus in 1660 Pococke translated into Arabic a book entitled *De veritate religionis Christianae*, written by the Dutch scholar Grotius for use by the Christian missionaries in the East Indies. The missionary purpose behind translating such a book into Arabic is clear. Further, at the request of Robert Huntington, who succeeded him as chaplain to the merchants of the Levant Company at Aleppo, he translated the Anglican liturgy and catechism into Arabic as a means of building bridges with the Christian Arabs. But this should not detract from his great achievements in the field of Arabic scholarship. He edited the Arabic text of Ibn Ṭufail's *Ḥayy ibn Yagdhān*, a twelfth century philosophical romance, based on a minor philosophical treatise by Avicenna, aiming at the reconciliation of reason and revelation. Growing up on a remote desert island, the hero – a child named Ḥayy ibn Yagdhān – arrives at conclusions similar to those of revealed faith. The Arabic text which Pococke edited was translated by his own son, Edward Pococke the younger (1648–1727), into Latin. Two English versions by George Keith and George Ashwell appeared in 1674 and 1686 respectively. In his *Apology for the True Christian Divinity* (1678) the Quaker apologist, Robert Barclay, discovers a striking affinity between the views expressed in *Ḥayy ibn Yagdhān* and the Quakers' notion of the inner light inside each individual. Referring to the 1674 English version of George Keith, Barclay states:

> There is a book translated out of the Arabick which gives an account of one Hai Ebn Yakdhān, who, without converse of man, living in an island alone, attained to such a profound knowledge of God, as to have immediate converse with him, and to affirm that the best and most certain knowledge of God is not that which is attained by premises promised, and conclusions deduced, but that which is enjoyed by conjunction of the mind of man with the Supreme Intellect

after the mind is purified from its corruptions, and is
separated from all bodily images, and is gathered into a
profound stillness.[26]

Ḥayy ibn Yagdhān is likewise thought to be the major source
for Robinson Crusoe and certainly influenced the 'autodi-
dactus' type of philosophical and speculative romance of
the eighteenth century. There is indeed an obvious correspondence in the description of the ways followed by both
Ḥayy and Crusoe to obtain food, clothes, and shelter. Man
versus nature is a central theme in each. Ibn Ṭufail's tale
has elements of the idea of the 'noble savage' later developed by Rousseau. Pococke also translated the Arabic
poem *Lamiyat al-Ajam* in 1661. In 1658–9 he published
his *Contextio Gemmarum*, a translation of Sa'īd al-Bitrīq's
(Eutychius) tenth century book *Naẓm al-Jawhar*.

Perhaps Pococke's greatest accomplishment as an
Arabist was his *Specimen Historiae Arabum*, published by
Oxford University in 1649. It contains the Arabic text and
Pococke's Latin translation of the *Dynasties* of Abu al-Faraj
(Bar Hebraeus), a Jacobite Syrian bishop. The text and the
translation occupy only thirty-one pages but Pococke then
adds over 350 pages of philological, historical, and theological notes. Those notes constitute a series of elaborate
essays on Arabic history, sciences, literature, and religion,
based upon detailed researches in over a hundred Arabic
manuscripts, and marking a key stage in the development of
Eastern studies. Pococke's translation and notes provided a
better and more accurate account of the rise of Islam than
any other contemporary English sources.

After a preface dedicated to John Selden, Pococke, based
on the account of Abu al-Faraj, surveys the pre-Islamic and

Islamic eras. He lists the various Arab tribes, the Arabs' excellence in astronomical knowledge and their literary skills, and goes in some detail into the life of Prophet Muḥammad, the miracle of the Qur'ān, and the various Islamic religious sects. Pococke's notes cover almost every aspect of Arab and Muslim life mentioned in the original Arabic text and are supported by information and quotations drawn from a variety of Muslim authors. An example which demonstrates Pococke's historical accuracy is his refutation, in his notes on Prophet Muḥammad's life, of several errors still prevalent in learned circles in Europe, including the Christian fable of the entombment of the Prophet in an iron coffin suspended between earth and heaven. More than anyone of his generation, Pococke provided fresh material on Muslim civilisation, relied on Muslim sources, and refuted many errors and fables about Islam current in his own time.

Holt sums up Pococke's achievement as an Arabist thus:

> His publications on Muslim history were not merely learned works but also in a restricted sense works of popularization. In the next century the process was to be carried further. Ockley was to write an English *History of the Saracens* and Sale was to produce an English version of the Koran preceded by a learned and detailed 'preliminary discourse'. Finally Gibbon was to integrate Muslim history with that of the Roman and Byzantine empires. These three writers still condition the thinking of the non-specialist on Islam and Muslim history and the image which they created, as their footnotes and references show, was largely derived from the pioneer work of Pococke. We are now in a third phase, when this image and the Muslim sources from which

it derives are being submitted to the techniques of
modern historical criticism but this should not obscure
the importance of the work of Pococke and the other
orientalists of the seventeenth and eighteenth centuries
in contributing to a better understanding of the Islamic
world and its history.[27]

Nevertheless, the medieval hostility towards Islam
continued into the sixteenth and seventeenth centuries.
The detailed historical facts presented by Pococke, and the
academic researches of other contemporary Arabists, seem
to have been isolated cases with no significant bearing on
the main development of false images of Islam and the East.

Lack of authentic material on Islam was not the sole
reason for the hostile Western attitude to Islam. As
Norman Daniel aptly puts it: 'Men seem to take it for
granted that an alien society is dangerous, if not hostile,
and the spasmodic outbreak of warfare between Islam and
Christendom throughout their history has been one mani-
festation of this. Apparently, under the pressure of their
sense of danger, whether real or imagined, a deformed
image of their enemy's beliefs takes shape in men's minds...
Doctrines that are the expression of the spiritual outlook of
an enemy are interpreted ungenerously and with prejudice,
even facts are modified – and in good faith – to suit the
interpretation.'[28]

A particular European state of mind with regard to Islam
had been formed in the Middle Ages, and it was to remain
(with few exceptions) virtually unchanged. Concurrently,
Islamic learning and culture, together with the influence of
ancient Greece and Rome, were steadily creating an intellectual climate in Europe that was to usher in the dawn

of the Renaissance and, consequently, the modern epoch. John Milton lived in a milieu which, while it owed much to Islamic civilisation, inherited and built on hostile and erroneous traditions directed against the faith of a people viewed as Europe's foremost enemies.

II

Milton's Knowledge of the Arabic Language and Islamic Heritage

The revival of interest in Arabic studies in early seventeenth century England arose from a combination of sheer commercial instinct and Protestant evangelical vehemence. Whereas the latter was, in a sense, a continuation of unsuccessful medieval Catholic attempts, the former was greatly enhanced by the establishment of the Turkey and East India Companies. Contacts in these two spheres of activity necessarily required a knowledge of the tongues and faith of the Muslim world. Naturally, it was the universities that took the lead in promoting Arabic studies.

At Cambridge, Abraham Wheelocke (also spelt Wheelock and Whelock) both taught and studied Arabic and was the most notable orientalist at Cambridge in Milton's day. He was elected a fellow of Clare College in 1619, and became university librarian in 1629, a job he held until his death in 1654. In 1631 Wheelocke persuaded a London city draper named Thomas Adams 'to defray the charge of an Arabic lecture at £40 per annum, for three years from Lady Day, 1632'. Consequently, a chair was founded at Cambridge and Wheelocke was appointed as the first professor of Arabic. Adams wrote to him on that appointment: 'I wish you much joy, in the execution of that hopeful employment, that you may be deservedly honored in Cambridge and renowned in England.'

The grant was made permanent in 1636. A letter of thanks, clearly stating the purposes of founding that chair, was addressed to Adams by the Vice-Chancellor and Heads of Colleges at Cambridge:

Worthy Sir,

Having these foure yeares enioyed your bountiful exhibition for the maintenaunce of a Professor of the Arabick tongue in our University, and now also understanding your pious desire of setling it for perpetuity; we cannot but returne you the Scholars tribute of thanks and honor due to so noble a Benefactor, and shall upon any intimation from you be ready to serve you with our best counsells and endeavors for the improving it to those good ends to which you intend it.

The work itselfe we conceive to tend not only to the advancement of good Literature by bringing to learned tongue; but also to the good service of the King and State in our commerce with those Easterne nations, and in God's good time to the enlarging of the borders of the Church, and propagation of Christian religion to them who now sit in darkness. The gentleman you have pitched upon for your Professor, Mr. Abraham Wheelocke, we do every way approve of, both for his abilities and for his faithful paynes and diligence in that employment.

God prosper the work according to your pious intentions; and render a full reward of it to you and yours; making your memory as the memories of all other our famous Benefactors, ever precious among us.[29]

Wheelocke was an accomplished Arabist. In Thomas Adams' letters to him, there are frequent references to his 'Arabic mill'; he became distinguished both as a student and a teacher and took an active part in drawing up the plan for Brian Walton's Polyglot Bible, 1654, in which he alone corrected the Arabic and Persian texts, 'his labours being interrupted only by his death'. Wheelocke was also an able and efficient librarian, and helped to make Cambridge University Library one of the most important centres of book collection in England. Henry Bradshaw (1831–86), an eminent Cambridge librarian for more than eighteen years, singled out Wheelocke's efforts for high praise.

The question which arises here is: did Milton know Wheelocke? There is no evidence I know of that he did, for Wheelocke's Arabic chair was founded just as Milton was leaving Cambridge (he took his MA on 3 July 1632, and then retired to Horton, about thirty-five miles from Oxford, for a life dedicated to private studies). But could Milton have known Wheelocke in the latter's capacity as a librarian? Harris Fletcher assumes that contact of a sort must have occurred:

> If Milton was able to use the books in the University library at all when a student, he must have known someone who could grant him access to them, and the person most likely to give him such access was Wheelock. Probably the first contact between Milton and Wheelock occurred while the latter was attempting to secure the post of librarian, that is, in 1627 or thereabouts. Almost anyone interested in books in any way, whether for their contents, as was Milton, or as commodities, would have known Wheelock, if in

Cambridge from 1625 onward, for Wheelock was doing everything possible to enable himself to make a living through any kind of academic connection.[30]

Obviously, Fletcher has no firm evidence that Milton knew or met Wheelocke. There is, however, an interesting instance where Milton's and Wheelocke's signatures appear together. Christopher Arnold, a German scholar who travelled in England in 1651 and met Milton, also briefly met John Greaves, who was an Arabic scholar at Oxford, and Wheelocke. Milton may never have met either Greaves or Wheelocke, but he may have known people who did. All three of them, Greaves, Wheelocke, and Milton, signed Arnold's album, now in the British Library. Another signatory of that album was Jacob Golius, Arabic scholar at Leiden, and friend of Greaves.

Indeed, there were Arabic manuscripts in the library of Cambridge University. The oriental collection of that university was based on the library of the famous Dutch scholar Erpenius. The duke of Buckingham was chancellor of Cambridge, and brought Erpenius' library from Leiden after a visit to The Hague in 1625–6. Buckingham was assassinated in 1623 and his widow gave the collection, consisting of eighty-five manuscripts, to Cambridge in 1632.

A second important collection, including twenty manuscripts obtained in Constantinople by Nicholas Hobart, was presented to Cambridge in 1655. There is also a letter, in manuscript form, dated 2 May 1632, from William Bedwell to Abraham Wheelocke, that renews a promise to bestow Bedwell's 'Alcoran' upon the university library. Other letters from John Clerke, Bedwell's son-in-law and a noted Arabist, refer to Bedwell's legacy of his Arabic lexicon to the University.

It has to be said, however, that all this interest in Arabic studies, and the collection of Arabic manuscripts, was occurring either as Milton was preparing to leave Cambridge or after he had actually left.

In 1635, about three years after his graduation from Cambridge, Milton was admitted as Master of Arts at the University of Oxford. Living at Horton, Milton might have benefited from the excellent library of that university, particularly the Bodleian collection. This assumption becomes more probable in the light of the fact that the Horton period was wholly devoted to reading and studies.

Oxford University received three important collections of oriental manuscripts in the seventeenth century. Archbishop Laud, as chancellor of the university, presented a great foundation collection, including hundreds of Arabic manuscripts. Interestingly, at this time Milton formed a close friendship with John Rouse, fellow of Oriel College and chief librarian of the Bodleian. That friendship continued for some time. In 1646 Milton presented a volume of tracts to Rouse. The presentation, in Latin, says (in Masson's English rendering):

> To the most learned and upright judge of books, John Rouse, Librarian of Oxford University, (who said this would please him), John Milton gladly sends these his pamphlets, to be received into that most ancient and celebrated library as into a temple of immortal fame and a vacation (as he hopes) exempt from envy and calumny, if Truth and Good Fortune alike be propitious.[31]

Again in 1647 Milton wrote Rouse an ode in Latin, in which he entertains the notion of immortality based on the preservation of the volume containing his minor poems in the library of Oxford University. In that ode, Milton addresses the little volume:

> You [the volume], it seems at last, were not empty, idle things, toils of mine, whatever my barren intellect poured forth. I am bidding you now, late though it be, to hope for a calm and quiet rest, a rest that shall be done with envy; I bid you hope for the blest abodes that kindly Hermes and the skilful guardianship of Rouse will vouchsafe you, abodes into which the wanton tongue of the rabble will not make its way, from which the throngs of worthless readers will speed afar. But our latest Children's children, and an age of sounder minds, will mayhap from heart untainted apply juster judgments to all things. Then when envy and malice shall be buried, if we deserve aught, the sound minds of after days will know it, thanks to Rouse's favour.[32]

It is clear that Milton was very well acquainted with the chief librarian of the Bodleian at a time when that library was receiving Arabic manuscripts. Another librarian Milton knew was Lucas Holstenius, who was the librarian of the Vatican when Milton was travelling in Italy (1638–9). As early as 1481, the Vatican library had a total of twenty-two codices 'in Arabico'. Recollecting his visit to that library, Milton states in a Latin letter to Holstenius (1639):

> When I went to the Vatican for the purpose of meeting you, you received me, a total stranger to you (unless

perchance anything had been previously said about me to you by Alexander Cherubini), with the utmost courtesy. Immediately admitted with politeness into the Museum, I was allowed to behold both the superb collection of books, and also very many manuscripts by Greek authors set forth with your explanations.[33]

The Italian humanists were pioneers in the field of Arabic studies. They collected, edited, and translated Arabic books, and were influenced by the great Islamic heritage of the Middle Ages. There is no record, however, that Milton met, during the course of his journey, any Italian Arabists. Interestingly, Milton shipped from Venice to England books that he had collected during his visit to Italy, some of which, Edward Philips (Milton's nephew) says, were 'curious and rare'. No mention is made of whether any of those 'curious and rare' books were in Arabic. Of course, the issue here is less to do with whether Milton had easy access to the Bodleian or to the Vatican collection, and more to do with whether he had any way of reading, or being read to, in the Arabic language.

I have been unable to find any evidence that Milton ever studied Arabic. The only reference in Milton to Arabic studies is in *The Christian Doctrine*. Writing on the unity of the trinity, he says that the passage in 1 John 5:7: 'There are three that bear record in heaven, the Father, the Word, and the Holy Ghost, and these three are one,' is 'wanting in the Syriac and the other two Oriental versions, the Arabic and the Ethiopic, as well as in the greater part of the ancient Greek manuscripts'.[34] As the footnote in the Yale edition to the reference indicates, it is most likely that Milton had the information about the Arabic text of the New Testament at second hand and not from any direct knowledge of his

own. Information about a lacuna in an Arabic translation
of the text of the New Testament was available in Brian
Walton's *Biblia Sacra Polyglota* (6 vols., London, 1654–7),
a publication which Milton had helped in various minor
ways, and in a variety of other references. The scholar who
edited and corrected this Arabic version in Brian Walton's
Polyglot Bible was none other than Abraham Wheelocke.

That none of Milton's tutors or instructors at St Paul's
School and at Christ's College knew Arabic lends an
added weight to the assumption that he never studied the
language. He did, however, know Hebrew and some Syriac.
(This Semitic language was the major language used by
Christian communities in the Middle East before Arabic
became dominant.) In Elegy 6, Milton mentions that
Thomas Young, his tutor at St Paul's School between 1618
and 1620, first taught him Hebrew.

Before entering university, graduates of St Paul's were
well instructed in Latin, Greek, and Hebrew, 'and sometimes in other Oriental tongues'.[35] Milton could definitely
read Hebrew in the Bible, and maybe a little in rabbinical
commentaries. Although not an expert Hebrew scholar,
he evidently possessed and used a copy of Brian Walton's
Polyglot Bible and also the great annotated Hebrew Bible
(*Mikraoth Gedoloth*) as edited by Johannes Buxtrof, the
elder (Basel, 1618–19). Writing in 1694, Edward Philips
tells us that soon after his return from Italy Milton took a
lodging in St Bride's churchyard where he began to tutor
his nephews. Naturally he began with:

> authors both of the Latin and Greek, and thus by
> teaching he in some measure increased his own knowl-
> edge, having the reading of all these Authors as it were by

Proxy; and all this might possibly have conduced to the preserving of his Eye-Sight, had he not, moreover, been perpetually busied in his own laborious undertakings of the Book or Pen. Nor did the Time thus studiously imployed in conquering the Greek and Latin Tongues, hinder the attaining of the chief Oriental languages, viz. The Hebrew, Caldee and Syriac, so far as to go through the Pentateuch, or Five Books of Moses in Hebrew, to make a good entrance into the Targum, or Chaldee Paraphrases, and to understand several Chapters of St. Matthew into the Syriac Testament.[36]

Milton's knowledge of Syriac may well have been confined to texts in which the language was printed in Hebrew characters instead of its regular script, since it was very rare then to print anything in Syriac letters. Although Philips refers to Milton's knowledge of the Chaldee tongue it was doubtful whether he really knew Aramaic, except what he could see printed alongside the Hebrew in his Bible. Thus, while we have some evidence as to the extent of Milton's knowledge of Hebrew, Syriac, and also Aramaic, there is nothing whatsoever to suggest that he knew Arabic.

While none of Milton's tutors was known for his knowledge of Arabic or for his interest in Arabic studies, Milton had friends who were either promoters of, or very much involved in, those studies, most prominently Samuel Hartlib and John Selden. Born in Germany of a Polish mother and an English father, Samuel Hartlib (c.1600–62) immigrated to England in 1628. In England, he contributed significantly to the improvement of agriculture, which won him a pension from Parliament, and to the cause of the unity of Protestant churches. Recognised as one of the virtuosi of his age, Hartlib was known for his interest in the improvement of education. His translation of Comenius' educational schemes under the title *A Reformation of Schools* (1642) stimulated Milton, among other writers, to respond in *Of Education* (1644), a work addressed to Hartlib himself. Milton also ends *Of Education* with an address to Hartlib:

> Thus, Mr. Hartlib, you have a general view in writing, as your desire was, oft that which at several times I had discoursed with you concerning the best and noblest way of Education; not beginning, as some have done, from the cradle, which yet might be worth many considerations.[37]

This friend of Milton was also known as a promoter of oriental learning. A twentieth century writer describes the praise Hartlib received from a distinguished orientalist:

> Abraham Wheelock, who was professor of Arabic and Librarian at Cambridge University, in letters to Hartlib, of which extracts are to be found among the papers in 1647 and later about his translation of the Alcoran into Greek and Latin and his intention to write notes in Arabic against the Alcoran, asked Hartlib to be a benefactor to the University by inducing lovers of virtue and learning to procure typographies for Arabic and Syriac and to cause a Maronite to be sent for, who is skilled in reading the hardest manuscripts in Arabic and Syriac and if possible in Persian.[38]

The fact that a friend of Milton was involved in the promotion of oriental studies, especially Arabic, raises many questions, but probably offers no answers. Did Hartlib involve his friend Milton in those endeavours? And, if not, was not Milton aware of Hartlib's efforts and their significance? The problem here is that we are not told whether Hartlib himself knew or studied Arabic. His role apparently resided in being a propagator of Arabic learning without being an Arabist himself. Lack of evidence as to Milton's knowledge of Arabic hampers our investigation from the start and casts serious doubt on any assumption pertaining to Milton's involvement in Hartlib's oriental schemes. But there is an important piece of information offered in the above passage – we are informed that Abraham Wheelocke asked Hartlib to help in providing typographies for Arabic and Syriac and in enlisting a Maronite to read hard manuscripts in the two languages. Can we infer that a possible acquaintance might have existed between Milton and Wheelocke as a result of Hartlib's knowledge of both men? Again, there is no documentary evidence to support this supposition. However, it is safe to say that Milton was probably quite aware of the scholarly activity in the field of Arabic studies that was going on in his own time. This possibility is reinforced in the light of Milton's relations with Selden.

Selden (1584–1654) was an accomplished student of Arabic, whose collection of manuscripts was rich in Hebrew and Arabic works. His interest in Semitic languages and learning lasted a lifetime:

> From his earliest years Selden found time to combine with his legal studies voluminous researches in oriental learning. For use in his oriental studies Selden made a collection of manuscripts and printed books, most of

which passed at his death into the Bodleian Library; he also had access to the manuscripts which Laud was procuring at great trouble and expense, and which were stored at Lambeth or presented to the University of Oxford.[38]

Two Semitic works by Selden – *De Diis Syris* (1617) and *Uxor Ebraica* or *Hebrew Wife* (1646) – were read by Milton, who used the former (especially in the catalogue of deities in Book 1 of *Paradise Lost*) and cited the latter to support his own conclusions in *The Doctrine and Discipline of Divorce*. Milton himself states that he read Selden's *Hebrew Wife*, on fornication as a cause for divorce, 'a question which has been copiously elucidated by our celebrated Selden in his *Hebrew Wife*',[39] and also makes clear that Selden's appeared two years after his, Milton's, discussion of the subject. In *Areopagitica*, Milton uses Selden's name to give an added weight to his defence of the freedom of the press:

> Whereof what better witness can ye expect I should produce than one of your own sitting in parliament, the chief of learned men reputed in this land, Mr. Selden; whose volume of natural and national laws proves, not only by great authorities brought together, but by exquisite reasons and theorems almost mathematically demonstrative, that all opinions, yea errors, known, read, and collated, are of main service and assistance toward the speedy attainment of what is truest.[40]

David Masson advances the idea that when Milton referred to Selden as 'our learned Selden' in *The Doctrine and Discipline of Divorce* (1643), it is quite possible that in

1643–4 he had just made Selden's personal acquaintance. Selden was then in his sixtieth year and Milton in his thirty-sixth. Whether the two men became intimate friends or not, it is clear that Milton both held Selden in high esteem and knew his works. Milton thus had an acquaintance who had attained a remarkable degree of competence in Semitic studies, both Hebrew and Arabic. Had Milton needed help in reading manuscripts or publications in Arabic, Selden would have been the scholar to offer that assistance. Unfortunately, the absence of any recorded evidence makes conclusions mere guesswork.

Although Milton did not apparently read or study Arabic, he did read works about Islam and Muslims. In addition to Christian polemic writings (treated in the Chapter I), Milton was also familiar with some travel literature about the Arab and Muslim world. There were two works which contain information about Muslims and Islam that Milton definitely read: Jean Bodin's *Colloquium Heptaplomeres* (1593) and Leo Africanus's *De totius Africae descriptione*.

Bodin (1530–96) was a French political philosopher and economist. Milton read two works by him. The first was entitled *De Republica*, Bodin's most important work, which is an argument favouring the exercise of absolute power as a necessity for effective government, with its only limits being divine or natural law. Milton mentions *De Republica* in the *Commonplace Book* as an argument in favour of divorce, and alludes to it in *The Reason of Church Government*.

The second Bodin work Milton read was *Colloquium Heptaplomeres*. Described as 'the most notorious, most sought after, and most difficult to procure in the seven-teenth century',[41] the book, which circulated secretly in manuscript form (it was first published in 1841), is a dialogue among seven men of learning from different religious persuasions. Those learned men eventually decide that they can live together in charity and toleration. Milton possessed a copy of the manuscript of that work, which he sent to some acquaintance in Germany. There are references to Milton's copy in letters exchanged between Christian von Boineburg, a diplomat, and Hermann Conring, a professor at the University of Helmstadt. In those letters, mention is made of Milton sending a copy of Bodin's manuscript to a friend in Germany. That friend has been identified as the Scottish presbyter James Dury (or Durie), a man who spent most of his life on the Continent attempting to unify the Protestant sects. During his residence in England, from 1640 to 1654, he had met Milton and became a member of his intimate circle. Dury and Milton had met perhaps as early as 1641 and certainly by 1644. *Colloquium Heptaplomeres* was a heretical attack against established religions and their institutions. The information Milton derived from this work about Islam certainly distorted further an already deformed image created by Christian polemic traditions.

There is some evidence that Milton knew the writings of the famous Arab historian, traveller and geographer Al-Ḥassan ibn Muḥammad al-Wazzan (c.1483–1550), known to Europeans as Leo Africanus, Jean Leon, or Leon L'Africain. Born in Granada, he finally settled in the Moroccan city of Fez. Al-Wazzan visited Egypt and Constantinople, and travelled extensively in Africa and the Middle East. Captured by Italian pirates near Djerba, an island off the coast of Tunisia, he was taken to Naples and then presented to Pope Leon X. Temporarily converted to Christianity, Al-Wazzan learned Latin and Italian (he already knew Hebrew and Spanish in addition to his native Arabic). Leon X, who was interested in Arabic studies himself, allowed Al-Wazzan to teach at the college of Bologna. After the death of his patron, Al-Wazzan befriended Cardinal Gilles de Niterbe, to whom he taught Arabic. He later returned to North Africa, reconverted to Islam, and died in Tunisia.

Al-Wazzan was a prolific writer. He wrote *A Biography of Arab Philosophers and Physicians* (in Latin), and compiled an Arabic-Latin-Hebrew medical dictionary. He also wrote a book on Islamic jurisprudence, a treatise on Islamic feasts, and another on Arabic syntax. He wrote in Italian, probably from Arabic drafts, *De totius Africae descriptione* and *De viris quibusdem illustribus apud Arabes*. The former was translated into many languages. The Latin version was produced by Jan Florian in 1556 and in 1600 John Pory translated it into English as *History and Description of Africa*.

Samuel Purchas incorporated most of the material in Pory's translation in Volume 6 of his *Purchas His Pilgrimes*; Milton read the 1632 Leiden reprint in Latin. Al-Wazzan's book served as the source for Milton's knowledge of the geography of North Africa and the history of its rulers. The reference to Almansor in *Paradise Lost* (2, 402–3) was most probably derived from Al-Wazzan's.

These indirect connections between Milton and the books and writers available in his time cannot demonstrate conclusively the sources of his references to Islam and the Orient. But I am trying to establish that a climate of discourse about the Orient existed from which Milton might have drawn. And the deeper one looks, the more suggestive the examples one finds.

In 1649, for example, Alexander Ross (1591–1654) published his English rendering of Du Ryer's French translation of the Qur'ān. Ross's version was suppressed on 19 March 1649; Milton had become Secretary for Foreign Tongues to the Council of State on 15 March, just four days earlier. Did Milton read Ross's translation? What role did he play in its suppression? It would have been strange for Milton, a lover of books and the seeker of all kinds of knowledge, not to have read it, and it would be interesting to know how Milton, the author of *Areopagitica*, who a few years earlier defended the freedom of the press, felt about its suppression. In *Areopagitica*, Milton opposes censorship on the ground of its hindrance of the progressive revelation of truth, and cites the example of 'the Turk':

> There is yet behind of what I purposed to lay open the incredible loss and detriment that this plot of licensing put us to. More than if some enemy at sea should stop up all our havens and ports and creeks, it hinders and retards the importation of our richest merchandise, truth. Nay. It was first established and put in practise by Antichristian malice and mystery, on set purpose to extinguish, if it were possible, the light of reformation, and to settle falsehood; little differing from that policy wherewith the Turk upholds his Alcoran, by the prohibition of printing. 'Tis not denied, but gladly confessed, we are to send our thanks and vows to Heaven, louder than most of nations, for that great measure of truth which we enjoy, especially in those main points between us and the Pope, with his appurtenances the prelates; but he who thinks we are to pitch our tent here, and have attained the utmost prospect of reformation that the mortal glass wherein we contemplate can show us, till we come to beatific vission, that

man by this very opinion declares that he is yet far short of truth.[42]

Furthermore, Ketton's Latin translation of the Qur'ān in the twelfth century was printed in Basel (1543) with a preface by Martin Luther himself. The holy book of Muslims was thus available in English and in Latin. The name and authority of Luther might well have been more than enough to lead Milton, the Protestant par excellence, to read a book introduced by that founder of Protestantism.

Milton was known for his habit of periodic self-scrutiny. It was his habit to pause at various intervals, reflecting on what he had accomplished and planning for future work. In *The Reason of Church Government*, for example, he tells his readers what he has so far accomplished and what he hopes to do in his future days. A man of such habits might, during one of his periodic pauses or moments of brooding, have thought that a knowledge of Islam's holy book would be indispensable for an understanding of the Muslim Turkish empire that was Christian Europe's most feared enemy. This supposition gains more credibility in the light of Milton's involvement in political and diplomatic activity in his capacity as Secretary for Foreign Tongues. Turkey was a major world power with which England had to deal, politically and commercially. First-hand knowledge of the faith of the Turks would have enriched the knowledge of a responsible government figure in charge of writing state letters to senior officials of other European countries which were, likewise, very much preoccupied with Turkish military might.

Edward Pococke, the foremost English Arabist of the seventeenth century, published his *Specimen Historiae*

Arabum in 1650 with a dedication to John Selden, Milton's friend. In addition to the Arabic text and a Latin rendering of the *Dynasties* of Abu al-Faraj (Bar Hebraeus), the work abounds in notes, explanations, and commentaries that cover numerous aspects of Arab and Muslim life. The appearance of this work, at a time when he was a government official, could have given Milton the valuable opportunity to learn more about the Arabs who were, as he puts it, the founders of the Turkish power: 'Nor should I overlook the fact that the Saracens [the Arabs], to whom the Turks mainly owe their existence, spread their power less by force of arms than by their interest in literature.'43 However, even if he did not read Pococke's work, Milton certainly read Leo Africanus' *History and Description of Africa*. Thus, in addition to the traditional polemic presentations of Muslims and Arabs with which Milton was indeed familiar, some straightforward historical information was available to him in Leo Africanus' work. He would also have found more authentic material, in Pococke's and other works as well, had he sought it.

John Milton always expressed an interest in knowing the wisdom and culture of other peoples; it is, after all, indispensable in that search for the truth Milton so cogently states in *Areopagitica*. The need for continual research and the necessity of knowing what others have accomplished in the endless fields of human learning are perhaps best expressed in *Paradise Regained*. The words Milton puts in Satan's mouth are:

> The Gentiles also know, and write, and teach
> To admiration, led by Nature's light;
> And with the Gentiles much thou must converse,

Ruling them by persuasion as thou mean'st,
Without their learning how wilt thou with them,
Or they with thee hold conversation meet?

(4, 227–32)

Milton's firm conviction in the importance of all human knowledge, Christian or otherwise, is one of the recurring themes in his works. Next to the Latin and Greek heritage in which Milton was more than adequately versed, Islamic learning boasts the largest array of works of knowledge. That heritage, too, was surely crucial in man's perpetual quest for the truth.

One of the extant versions of the New Testament was in Arabic (Milton refers to it in *The Christian Doctrine*). The Psalms were also printed in Arabic. Leo Miller reports on a book written by Isaac Casaubon, a well-known scholar of the time of James I, whose son, Meric Casaubon, was a contemporary of John Milton and also a noted scholar. The book was *Psalterium Hebreum, Grecum, Arabicum et Chaldeum cum tribus Latinis interpretationis et glossis*, printed in Genoa by Porro, in 1516, and edited by Agostino Giustiniani. This book seems to be a very early Arabic printing of the Psalms. Although a translator of the Psalms himself, Milton never mentioned seeing any Arabic version. However, this printing and the Arabic version of the New Testament clearly indicate the availability of biblical material in Arabic. Milton might never have read or studied the language (for there is no proof he ever did), but he certainly had friends who were either Arabists themselves (such as Selden) or who supported and encouraged those involved in this kind of study. There was, therefore, always the possibility of having someone who knew Arabic explain the contents of a book to him. The availability of an Arabic printing of the Psalms can even help in the effort to learn that language: one way to learn a new language is to read a work that reproduces very familiar material, such as the Psalms, in the new language.

III

Oriental References in Milton's Works

1. Arabia

There are some references in Milton's works to Arabia, gleaned from a variety of sources ranging from the Bible to classical historical accounts and European travel narratives. According to the political layout of the region in the first century AD, Arabia was divided into Arabia Felix (free Arabia), Arabia Deserta (the part controlled by Persia), and Arabia Petraea (Roman controlled Arabia). Arabia Felix is usually singled out as the blessed Arabia, land of plenty and beauty. It occupies the southern parts of the Arabian Peninsula where four states were known to have established themselves: Ma'in, Saba, Qataban, and Ḥadramaut. The Sabaeans built an advanced agricultural society, centring on Ma'rib (in modern Yemen). Because of their control of the overland trade routes, they became masters of Arabia Felix.

The basic commodity in which the Sabaeans traded was frankincense, which was very much in demand for rituals in Egypt, Mesopotamia, Greece, and Rome. Frankincense was grown (or collected) in the Mahra and Dhofar regions. The proverbial wealth of Arabia Felix is referred to in 1 Ezekiel 27:19–27. The Queen of Sheba, who wanted to test the wisdom of King Solomon (which she discovered to be profound), presented that Hebrew king with spices, gold,

and precious stones (1 Kings 10:1–13). The gold of Arabia
Felix was even used for gilding the Temple. Tradition had
it that the queen married Solomon, and that the Ethiopian
royal line descended from that nuptial union. A land of
luxury, perfume, and beauty, Arabia Felix was thought to
contain the biblical Garden of Eden. Milton compares
Satan's sensations on his approach to the prelapsarian
Paradise with those of sailors, after rounding the Cape
of Good Hope, upon smelling the wind-blown odours of
Arabia the blessed:

> And higher than that Wall a circling row
> Of goodliest Trees loaden with fairest Fruit,
> Blossoms and Fruits at once of golden hue
> Appear'd, with gay enamell'd colors mixt:
> On which the Sun more glad impress'd his beams
> Than in fair Evening Cloud, or humid Bow,
> when God hath show'rd the earth; so lovely seem'd
> That Lantskip: And of pure now purer air
> Meets his approach, and to the heart inspires
> Vernal delight and joy, able to drive
> All sadness but despair: now gentle gales
> Fanning their odoriferous wings dispense
> Native perfume, and whisper whence they stole
> Those balmy spoils. As when to them who sail
> Beyond the *Cape of Hope*, and now are past
> *Mozambic*, off at Sea North-East winds blow
> Sabean Odors from the spicy shore
> Of Araby the blest, with such delay
> Well pleas'd they slack thir course, and many a league
> Cheer'd with the grateful smell old Ocean smiles.
>
> (*PL* 4, 146–165)

The notion that winds of Arabia pass out to sea 'laden
with balmy odours' had been prevalent from the time of
Herodotus. Milton's lines were also traced back to Diodorus
Siculus's *Bibliotheca Historia*, a book Milton had in his own
library. Diodorus claims that sailors, passing the Cape of
Good Hope northward, smell the fragrance of Arabia Felix
while far away at sea:

> The next *Arabians* are named Carbes, and adjoyning
> to them are the Sabeans, the most populous Nation
> of all that inhabit Arabia the happy, and replenished
> with all things which we esteeme to be most pretious,
> ... In Sweete odours, which naturally are produced
> for their Countrey, they surpasse all other Reggions
> of the World; for *Balsamum* growes in the *Maritime*
> part thereof, and *Cassia* likewise; as also another
> Hearb of a singular vertue ... In the *Mediterranean* part
> thereof are many goodly Forrests, full of Trees bearing
> Frankincense, and Myrrhe; therin grow also Palm-
> trees, Canes, Cinamon, and other such like odoriferous
> things. Whereof it is not possible to recount all the
> severall sorts in particular, so abundantly hath Nature
> assembled them there together; so that the odours,
> which come to our sences from those Trees, seeme to be
> somewhat is truly Divine ... And certainly such as saile
> in those Seas (though they be farre from the Continent)
> partake in the pleasure of those sweet smells; for the
> winds, which in the Spring time blow from the Land,
> transport such odours to the Maritime parts therabout;
> for the vertue of those Aromaticks is not weake and
> faint, but so strong and fresh, as it pierces through all
> our senses; so that the winde, in such sort mingled

with delicate Savors, blowing upon the Sea, affects the spirits of passengers with a mervialous sweetnesse, and greatly avails unto health: For this so odoriferous an aire proceeds not from Aromaticks brayed in a Morter, but from the very Country and Trees themselves, to which it is proper as it were by a certaine Divine nature, so as unto them, who smell such odours, it seems to be that very Ambrosia, whereof the Fables speake, and indeed one cannot give a more proper terme to so great an excellency of sweet smells.[44]

A.W. Verity corrects Milton's north-east by making it 'rather north according to modern geography'.[45] Robert Cawley insists on a north-easterly direction: 'Many contemporary maps show Mozambique distinctly southeast of Arabia, so that "north" would have been positively wrong. Heylyn in *Cosmographie* (London, 1652), for instance, in his maps of Africa proves that ships which are "past Mozambic" would depend on northeasterly breezes if they were to enjoy the fragrance of Arabia Felix.'[46]

We should not worry ourselves about Milton's geographical precision and exactness. Nothing would be more irrelevant than to demand of a poet to be a geographer. Milton the artist enjoys the sheer strangeness of names, their remoteness, and their exotic evocations. Arabia Felix offers Milton a frame of poetic reference that heightens the reader's awareness of distance, of wild romantic beauty, and imaginative flights and sublimity. To the inhabitants of noisome London such descriptions of perfumed winds offer a sense of relief and comfort. Arabia Felix thus serves as an analogue to the prelapsarian Paradise. There are trees laden with 'fairest Fruit' and the sheer charm of the place is reminiscent of Milton's portrayal of the paradise that Satan is intent on destroying. 'Fruit' is really one of the most important words, images, and symbols in *Paradise Lost*. Both Arabia Felix and the Garden of Eden, as Milton depicts them in his epic, have scented fruits that arouse human senses. As an image, Edenic fruits are 'savoury fruits, of taste to please/True appetite...' (*PL* 5, 304–05). The emphasis is on the taste and smell of the fruit. The smell mingles with those of frankincense and myrrh to create an atmosphere of delight, happiness, and even holiness, not to be found except in the Garden of Eden and in Arabia Felix. However, by implication, the image of a scented fruit is transformed into a metaphor and is ultimately crystal-lised into a symbol. That scented fruit simply becomes the forbidden fruit of the tree of knowledge on whose taste or touch the fate of the whole of mankind depends. Fruits, spices, and flowers also symbolise Eve's loveliness, frailty, and vulnerability. In the crucial temptation scene in Book 9 of *Paradise Lost*, Satan, anxious to find Eve alone, spies the mother of mankind.

> Veil'd in a Cloud of Fragrance, where she stood,
> Half Spi'd, so thick the Roses bushing round
> About her glow'd, oft stooping to support
> Each flow'r of slender stalk, whose head though gay
> Carnation, Purple, Azure, or speckt with Gold,
> Hung drooping unsustain'd, them she upstays
> Gently with Myrtle band, mindless the while,
> Herself, though fairest unsupported Flow'r,
> From her best prop so far, and storm so nigh.
>
> (425–32)

Satan is the storm which destroys those flowers; a violent scattering of innocence and beauty. However, this annihilation of harmony and beauty develops into a paradox, similar to the famous *felix culpa*. The destruction of petals and roses makes way, in the process of nature and the cycle of time, for the birth of other flowers. The catalyst in bringing about this process is the 'scented fruit' itself. Geoffrey Hartman calls the attention of Milton's readers to a counterplot subtly interwoven in the similes and images of *Paradise Lost*;[47] in order for fruitfulness – both literal and metaphorical – to be a reality, other fruits and flowers should be picked and scattered. Christ speaks of salvation in terms of bringing forth fruits of 'more pleasing savour':

> See Father, what first Fruits on Earth are sprung
> From thy implanted Grace in Man, these Sighs
> And Prayers, Which in this golden censer, mixt
> With Incence, I thy Priest before thee bring
> Fruits of more pleasing savor from thy seed
> Sown with contrition in his heart, than those
> Which his own hand manuring all the Trees
> Of Paradise could have produc't, ere fall'n
> From innocence.
>
> (*PL* ii, 22–30)

Arabia Felix provides an earthly analogue and a parallel to the religious-poetic vision of the unfallen Garden of Eden.

Milton describes the sweet odours of Arabia in such a way as to elicit an almost sensuous response on the part of readers. Satan, recognising the intoxicating effect of the Arabian winds, tempts Christ with food, women, and all

possible bodily delights to be consummated in an atmosphere 'Of chiming strings or charming pipes, and winds/
Of gentlest gale Arabian odors fann'd/From their soft wings,
and *Flora*'s earliest smells' (*PR* 2, 263–5). In 'Elegia Quinta',
written in Milton's twentieth year and entitled 'In adventum
verts' (On the Coming of Spring), Mother Earth is described
as breathing 'the perfume of Arabian harvest'. Milton's fond-
ness for synaesthesia is characteristic of his poetry. Helen
Gardner rightly remarked that Milton's paradise 'is a paradise of all the senses'.[48] G. Wilson Knight says that Milton's
'use of smell and taste is probably more abundant than that of
any English poet but Keats'.[49]

On his way to Paradise looking for Adam and Eve, Satan
stops in the sun (to ask the angel Uriel about his course).
Milton describes the sun in words that recall Diodorus'
account of Arabia:

> What wonder then if fields and regions here
> Breathe forth Elixir Pure, and Rivers run
> Potable Gold, when with one virtuous touch
> Th' Arch-Chemic Sun so far from us remote
> Produces with Terrestrial Humor mixt
> Here in the dark so many precious things
> Of color glorious and effect so rare?
>
> (*PL* 3, 606–12)

Diodorus points out that the sun works wonders in Arabia.
He goes on to say that there is a world of precious stones
of different natures 'as well in colour as splendor… and the
heat of the Sunne gives to stones that colour of gold which
they have'.[50] Noticeable here is the visual image which,
when added to the sense of smell in the previously quoted

lines (*PL* 4, 146–65), intensifies and heightens the sensuousness of the Arabian atmosphere.

The association of Arabia Felix with perfume and luxury became a commonplace poetic reference in the English literature of the sixteenth and seventeenth centuries. Fletcher speaks of 'the sweetness of Arabian wind, sun blowing/Upon the treasure of perfume and spices' (*The Bloody Brother*, 5.3). Massinger compares the sweetness of Lidia's breath to the 'smooth gales that glide o'er happy Araby' (*The Great Duke of Florence*, 2.3). Macbeth's sin, as Shakespeare describes it, cannot be sweetened by 'all the perfumes of Arabia' (*Macbeth*, 5.1.25). In Chapman's *Bussy d'Amboise* (5.4.100–1) we have the following two lines: 'Haste thee where the grey ey'd perfumes/Her rosy chariot with Sabaean spices.' Another widespread reference at those times was to the legendary phoenix whose abode was thought to be in Arabia Felix. Milton compares Samson to this 'self-begott'n bird':

> In the Arabian woods embost
> That no second knows nor third,
> And lay ere while a Holocaust,
> From out her ashy womb now teem's,
> Revives, reflourishes, then vigorous most
> When most unactive deem'd,
> And though her body die, her fame survives,
> A secular bird ages of lives.

The Christian ritualistic symbolism evoked by the association of Samson with the phoenix is a critical commonplace in Milton's scholarship.[51] The legend of the phoenix is also referred to in *Paradise Lost* (5, 270–4). Interestingly, this bird prepares for its death and subsequent resurrection by burning itself in a splendid pyre of spices. Ovid, Milton's most likely source in this respect, says:

> It [the Phoenix] does not live on seeds and green things, but on the gum of frankincense and the juices of amomum. This bird, forsooth, when it has completed five centuries of his life, builds for itself a nest in the topmost branches of a waving palm-tree, using his talons and his clean beak; and when he has covered this over with cassiabark and light spikes of nard, broken cinnamon and yellow myrrh, he takes his place upon it and so ends its life amidst the odours. And from his father's body, so they say, a little phoenix springs up which is destined to attain the same length of years. When age has given him strength, and he is able to carry burdens, he relieves the tall palm's branches of the heavy nest, piously bears his own cradle and his father's tomb through the thin air, until, having reached the city of the Sun, he lays the nest down before the sacred doors of the Sun's temple.[52]

Nevertheless, Arabia is not only the splendid, affluent, and mysterious southern part. There is also Arabia Deserta, the barren and inhospitable northern region of the peninsula. Writing of Arabia Felix more than a century after Milton's death, Gibbon stated that 'the splendid colouring of fancy and fiction has been suggested by contrast [to Arabia Deserta] and heightened by distance'.[53] In Milton's *Paradise Regained*, Jesus Christ looks south to the 'inaccessible... Arabian drought' (3, 247), and in 'Elegia Quarta', which Milton wrote when he was just eighteen years old,

and addressed to his tutor Thomas Young, there is a reference to 'the Tishbite prophet [Elijah] … [who] walked the
byways of the desert with unaccustomed steps and trod the
rough sands of Arabia [*Desertasque Arbum* in Milton's original Latin] when he fled from the hands of King Ahab'.[54]
The lady's lines (207–9) in *Comus* bring to mind Arabia
Deserta:

> A thousand fantasies
> Begin to throng into my memory,
> of calling shapes and beck'ning shadows dire,
> And airy tongues that syllable men's names
> On Sands and Shores and desert Wildernesses.

The lady's lines echo numerous descriptions of the Arabian
wilderness, such as that of Marco Polo's journey, of Friar
Odoric's as narrated by Hakluyt, and of Mandeville's
Vale Perilous (not to mention the paraphrases of
cosmographers).

Associated with the inhospitable wilderness of the
Arabian deserts is the Dead Sea with its bitter harvest of
ashy fruits. After Satan and his followers were transformed
into serpents, they – hungry and thirsty – began to pluck

> The Fruitage fair to sight, like that which grew
> Near that bituminous Lake where *Sodom* flam'd:
> This more delusive, not the touch, but taste
> Deceiv'd: they fondly thinking to allay
> Their appetite with gust, instead of Fruit
> Chew'd bitter Ashes, which th' offended taste
> With spattering noise rejected: oft they assay'd
> Hunger and thirst constraining, drugg'd as oft,

With hatefullest disrelish writh'd thir jaws
With soot and cinders fill'd; so oft they fell
Into the same illusion, not as Man
Whom they triumph'd, once lapst.

(*PL* 10, 561–72)

The bitter ashes of fruits growing on the banks of this
'Asphaltic Pool' (*PL* 1, 411) echo the biblical references to
the vines of Sodom: 'Their vine is of the vine of Sodom, and
of the fields of Gomorrah: their grapes are grapes of gall,
their clusters are bitter' (Deut. 23:23). Milton's description
also owes much to various accounts dispersed in popular
encyclopedias and in the travel literature of that time.

The Dead Sea was called 'Lake Asphalites'. Diodorus
was thought to have been the one who gave it this name,
which Sandys used when he referred to 'that cursed lake
Asphalites: so named of the Bitumen which it Vomiteth'.[55]
Sir Walter Raleigh had a similar description in his *History
of the World*: 'As it is found by Experience that those
Pomegranates, and other Apples, or Oranges, which do still
grow on the Banks of this cursed lake, do looke fair, and are
of good Colour on the outside; but being cut, have nothing
but dust within.'[56]

2. Ormuz

The building of Pandemonium not only offers Satan the
opportunity to display his vain glory, but also provides those
devils with a meeting place for consultations, disputations,
and decision-making. The council head, Satan, opening the
meeting, sits pompously

High on a throne of royal state, which far
Outshone the wealth of *Ormuz* and of Ind,
Or where the gorgeous East with richest hand
Show'rs on her kings *Barbaric* Pearl and Gold,

(*PL* 2, 1–4)

Ormuz (Arabic Hurmuz) is situated at the mouth of the Persian Gulf. As a crucial spot on the world's strategic map, Ormuz had always enjoyed a virtual monopoly over the movement of sea traffic into and out of the gulf. At present, it controls the shipments of Arabian and Iranian oil to the world. During the Renaissance, the importance of Ormuz was recognised by the European sea powers and by Turkey and Persia. A Portuguese naval officer named Alfonso de Albuquerque made it tributary to the king of Portugal in October 1507. He built a fort there, but did not complete it because of the resistance of some local tribal chiefs and because of the desertion of some Portuguese as well. It was in 1515 that Ormuz was firmly seized, thus giving the Portuguese 'the key to the Persian Gulf' and securing their trade with Persia and Arabia. However, because of intense commercial competition the city was virtually destroyed in 1622 by the English and the Persians.

Due to its control of the sea trade route into the Persian Gulf, Ormuz became a symbol of wealth and luxury, similar to Arabia Felix. Milton had this in mind when he compared Satan's throne to the riches of Ormuz. Andrew Marvell, Milton's contemporary and acquaintance, speaks of the pomegranates of Bermuda which 'enclose jewels richer than Ormuz shows'.[57] Ben Jonson likewise speaks of a ship coming from Ormuz laden with drugs (*Alchemist*, 1.2.59). Fulke Greville made Ormuz the scene of his play

Alaham, and perhaps some of Milton's readers responded
to the name by recalling the cry of the usurping hero in the
last scene:

> Is this Ormuz? Or is Ormuz my hell,
> Where only furies, and not Men, doe dwell?[58]

Ormuz's wealth was also described by a number of travellers, and Sir Thomas Herbert thought it deserved the
following tribute:

> If all the world were but a Ring
> Ormuz the Diamond should bring.[59]

John W. Draper suggests that 'it is possible, perhaps only
possible, that he [Milton] took his comparison of Satan's
diamond throne with the "wealth of Ormuz" from an
Arabian proverb quoted in de Mandelslo's Voyages: "If the
world were a Ring, Ormuz ought to be considered as the
Diamond in it".'[60]

3. Gaza

That Milton relied for his references to places in the Holy
Land on the biblical account hardly needs elaboration. The
Bible, particularly the Old Testament, was Milton's main
source for the map of Palestine and adjacent realms. The
Palestine that Milton described was thus the pre-Islamic
region vividly portrayed in Holy Writ. However, he occasionally mixes the biblical accounts with those of contemporary travellers, blending the old with the new and linking

the past with the present. This technique of using a modern traveller to bring up to date, so to speak, traditional material came with Milton to be common practice. The portrayal of Gaza is a case in point.

Milton's dramatisation of the war between Samson and the Philistines begins with Samson 'eyeless at Gaza' in the hands of his foes. Gaza was a principal city comprising Gath, Ekron, Ashdod, and Ashkolon, the country of Philistia (a name given to the south-western coastal plain of Palestine). According to the Old Testament these five cities, known as the Pentapolis, were settled by the sons of Caphtor (the Hebrew name for Crete). Delilah, Samson's wife[61] and a Philistine herself, justifies on patriotic grounds her collaboration with her countrymen in capturing Samson. In her famous farewell speech to her husband, she expresses her joy at becoming a heroine who will be celebrated in all the cities of the Philistines:

> My name perhaps among the circumcis'd
> In *Dan, in Judah*, and the bordering tribes,
> To all posterity may stand defam'd,
> With malediction mention'd, and the blot
> Of falsehood most unconjugal traduc't.
> But in my country were I most desire!
> In Ekron, Gaza, Asdod, and in Gath
> I shall be nam'd among the famousest
> Of women, sung at solemn festivals,
> Living and dead recorded, who to save
> Her country from a fierce destroyer, chose
> Above the faith of wedlock bonds, my tomb
> With odors visited and annual flowers.

(*SA*, 975–87)

Samson likewise views himself as a deliverer of his people from what is called the 'Philistian yoke'. Aware of such a role, he clearly states:

> Promise was that I
> Should Israel from Philistian Yoke deliver;
> Ask for this great deliverer now, and find him
> Eyeless in *Gaza* at the Mill with slaves,
> Himself in bonds under Philistian yoke.   (38–42)

The whole work focuses on the episode of Samson's captivity, which ends in his pulling the temple down on the assembled Philistines and on himself. The English traveller George Sandys (1578–1644) states that he saw columns in ruins (apparently a Roman amphitheatre) at Gaza. Milton might have been influenced by Sandys' account of those ruins:

> On the North-East Corner and summit of the Hill are the ruines of huge Arches sunk low in the Earth, and other foundations of a stately Building... The Jews do fable this place to have been the Theatre Sampson pulled down on the heads of the Philistines.[62]

Sandys, who left England in 1610 on an extended tour of France, Italy, and the Middle East, stayed for a year in Turkey, Egypt, and Palestine. His visit to the Holy Sepulchre in Jerusalem inspired 'A hymn to my Redeemer' – an outburst of fervent verse, which gave Milton hints for his 'Ode on the Passion' (stanza vii). Milton's reference to a cave where Christ lodged (*PR* 1, 307) might also have been suggested by Sandys' description of the reputed cave of John the Baptist in the wilderness.

4. Al Mansor

Following the example of Virgil in Book 6 of *The Aeneid*, when the future of Rome was foretold in a prophetic manner, Milton made Michael lead Adam in Book 11 of *Paradise Lost* to the top of a high hill in Paradise in order to survey 'the Hemisphere of Earth'. Adam saw the future of man passing before his eyes. He also saw various countries, kingdoms, and places, including

> Atlas Mount
> The Kingdoms of Almansor, Fez and Sus,
> Morocco and Algiers, and Tremisen.
>
> (*PL* 2, 402–4)

To whom was it that Milton referred as 'Almansor'? Different Muslim caliphs and rulers have been suggested as possible candidates. The problem of identifying the person Milton had in mind was rendered more complex by the word itself. Almansor (Arabic Al-Mansūr) is an epithet, meaning 'the victorious', that was attached to the names of numerous caliphs and leaders as a title of honour and dignity. Masson was the first to suggest that Milton meant the Abbasid Caliph Abu Ja'fer ibn Muḥammad (754–75), an opinion Verity favours.[63] Masson and Verity did not, however, specify Milton's source of information on Abu Ja'fer. Moreover, that Abbasid caliph had Baghdad (a city he himself built) as his capital. Thus while the heart of Abbasid political activity lies in the Arab East, the places Milton mentions are all in North Africa (the Arab West). Historically, the North African territories were nominally part of the Abbasid Caliphate; in reality they enjoyed a kind of semi-autonomous status. Had Milton intended Abu Ja'fer, he would have made Michael show Adam the territories adjacent to the centre of the Abbasid rule, where that caliph's power is most obviously seen and directly exercised. The choice of locations in the far north of Africa would have been inappropriate.

More recent editors have settled on Ibn Abi Amīr Muḥammad (939–1002), who was the chief minister of Hisham II (976–1009), the Umayyad Caliph of Cordoba. A choice of a chief minister is unfortunate. Ibn Abi Amīr was not a ruler in his own right, but rather a senior government official under the caliph. Moreover, none of the places Milton mentions is located in Spain, where Ibn Abi Amīr held his ministerial office.

A third candidate has been Abū Tahīr Ismā'īl ibn Obeidullah al-Mahdī (914–53), the third caliph of the Obeidiyyeh Fatimids. He was known as a firm caliph who put down a number of mutinies and rebellions against his rule. Having Al-Mahdiyyeh (in Tunisia) as his capital, Abū Tahīr controlled Algiers and much of Morocco. It is clear that Abū Tahīr's main sphere of activity was in Tunisia, while the places Milton mentions are in Algeria and Morocco.

In an interesting paper, Gordon Campbell and Roger Collins[64] advance the thesis that Milton's Almansor was no other than the Almohad Emīr Abū Yūsuf Ya'qūb al-Mansūr (r.1184–99), the only Al-Mansur mentioned by Al-Ḥassan ibn Muḥammad al-Wazzan (Leo Africanus) whose *History and Description of Africa* Milton certainly read, 'in the Latin version, in its 1632 Leiden reprinting'. This suggestion gains more weight in the light of the many accounts in Leo Africanus' book of Fez, Morocco, and Tremisene. Abū Yūsuf was also a large enough figure to merit a mention by

Milton. He was only twenty-five when he assumed power. As a young and energetic caliph, Abū Yūsuf opened a new era in the history of Al-Maghreb (Arab North Africa) and Muslim Spain. He initiated various reforms in the religious and social spheres; one of those was to give judges the right to examine the decisions made by his own viceroys. He had to fight a dangerous mutiny led by Ibn Ghaniyeh. After the defeat of the latter, Abū Yūsuf became the undisputed ruler of all of North Africa and Spain. He then started his military campaigns against the Franks, who had already seized four cities from the Muslims in Spain. Alfonso of Toledo feared the might of Abū Yūsuf and, consequently, sought a peace treaty with him that lasted for four years. Ultimately, the Franks attacked but were repelled and decisively defeated in 1196. After his victories in Spain, Abū Yūsuf returned to Morocco, where he died. The battles he waged in Spain against the Franks in the west were, in a sense, an extension of Saladin's war against the crusaders in the east. A character of such importance would have attracted Milton's historical awareness and captured his poetic imagination. Abū Yūsuf may or may not have been Milton's Almansor. However, the very name of Almansor evokes a sense of manliness and courage as well as a set of other military virtues that may justify Milton's choice of the name.

5. The Ottoman Turks

For more than five centuries (roughly from the middle of the fourteenth century until 1918), Ottoman Turkey was the dominant Muslim power facing Christian Europe. Not only was it a deterrent against renewed Crusades, but it also represented a formidable military threat to the very survival of Europe itself. The memories of the Crusades, the missionary zeal against an alien faith, and the military might of the Ottoman Empire had all contributed to the creating of Europe's anti-Ottoman prejudices. To the Europe of the late Middle Ages and of the Renaissance, Turkey simply stood for the forces of the Anti-Christ, hampering the restoration of the lost Eden and the establishment of God's kingdom on Earth. Religious difference, hatred, suspicion, and sheer fear had thus created a fervent dogmatic attitude towards Ottoman Turkey as an embodiment and a representative of a set of values Europe was determined to oppose. Milton's references to Turkey must be viewed within this context of traditional enmity and religious dogma. To him, Turkey is a living symbol of 'tyranny' and 'servitude', lacking in rational supremacy and self-restraint. In *Eikonoklastes*, he draws a parallel between British subjects under Charles I and Turks under a sultan. The rule of Charles I is described as a 'Turkish Tyranny, that spurn'd down those Laws, which gave it life and being so long as it endur'd to be regulated Monarchy'. In *Articles of Peace*, Milton attacks what he calls the 'plain Turkish Tyranny' some Christian kings tried to impose on their people:

> Neither is it any new project of the Monarchs, and their Courtiers in these dayes, though Christians they would be thought, to endeavour the introducing of a plain Turkish Tyranny. Witnesse that Consultation had in the Court of *France* under *Charles* the ninth at *Blois*, where in Poncet, a certain Court projector, brought in secretly by the Chancellor *Biragha*, after many praises of the Ottoman Government; proposes means and ways at large in presence of the King, the

Queen Regent, and *Anjou* the King's Brother how with best expedition, and least noyse the Turkish Tyranny might be set up in *France*.[65]

'Turkish Tyranny' is carefully distinguished from traditional (regulated) or constitutional monarchy. The Turkish example represents an extreme case of absolute dictatorship where all the 'natural' rights of people are ignored. Charles I of England and Charles IX of France were, according to Milton, guilty of turning constitutional monarchy into Turkish despotism. Again in the *Commonplace Book*, Milton points to the example of Charles IX of France:

Thuanus tells us that King Charles IX, the Queen-Mother, and others took counsel together at Blois to make the French monarchy a Turkish tyranny; and he gives at length the very cogent arguments for doing this as set forth by a certain Poncetus.[66]

Milton always maintains that a king should be differentiated from a tyrant. This point is plainly stated in, among other works of Milton, the *Second Defence of the English People* (1652):

If I inveigh against tyrants, what is this to Kings? Whom I am far from associating with tyrants. As much as an honest man differes from a rogue, so much I contend that a king differes from a tyrant. Whence it is clear that a tyrant is so far from being a king that he is always in direct oppostion to a king. And he who peruses the records of history, will find that more kings have been subverted by Tyrants than by their subjects.

He therefore who would authorize the destruction of tyrants does not authorize the destruction of kings, but of the most inveterate enemies to kings.

In *Paradise Lost* (1, 349), Satan is referred to as a Turkish Sultan. Regardless of the deceptive show of democracy and freedom he puts on in the famous council scene, he emerges, as he really is, a despot. After Satan's seconding of Beelzebub's proposal – actually Satan's – that the only possible revenge against God is the temptation of the 'human pair', the narrator immediately comments in the following manner:

> Thus saying rose...
> Prudent, lest from his resolution rais'd
> Others among the chief might offer now
> (Certain to be refus'd) what erst they fear'd;
> And so refus'd might in opinion stand
> His Rivals, winning cheap the high repute
> Which he through hazard huge must earn.
>
> (2, 466–73)

The analogy between Satan and a Turkish tyrant is strengthened further by Milton's likening of the devils' council to a Turkish Divan:

> Thir mighty Chief return'd: loud was th' acclaim:
> Forth rush'd in haste the great consulting Peers,
> Rais'd from thir dark Divan, and with like joy
> Congratulant approach'd him, who with hand
> Silence, and with these words attention won.
>
> (10, 454–8)

Divan (Arabic *dīwan*) is a meeting place, a regal or imperial court. The expression of other views at this 'divan' is not tolerated since authority is arbitrarily and capriciously exercised.

Milton never lost sight of the fact that Turkey was Europe's foremost adversary. Defining holy war, he says: 'Of holy warre as they call it: To fight with Turks & Saracens.' Milton here distinguishes Turks from Saracens (Arabs). The same distinction also occurs in 'Prolusion 7':

> *What can we say if our opponents put before us the argument that the modern Turks, ignorant of all literature, have obtained the mastery of affairs widely throughout the opulent kingdoms of Asia?*
>
> Truly, in that state (if indeed that ought to be call'd a state in which the power has been continuously usurped by force and murder on the part of the most cruel men whom a union of wickedness has brought together in one place) I have heard of nothing that may be within it noteworthy as a model... *Nor, to be sure, would I forget that the Saracens, in a sense the founders of the Turkish power, extended their dominion not more by devotion to arms than to good literature.*[67] (Author's italics)

In an age that did not really distinguish Turk from Saracen, Milton's distinction is noteworthy and indicates a familiarity with the details of Arab and Muslim history. The Arabs had Milton's admiration because they spread their dominions, according to him, not by mere military force but by literature and works of learning and culture. Such praise implies a recognition of the importance of Arabic literature and its influence on other people and other cultures.

By contrast, the Turks are 'ignorant of all literature'. They gained mastery, as Milton puts it, by naked force. Such a blind primitive force makes slaves of its people and renders them incapable of achieving any cultural prominence. In *Areopagitica* Milton tells the assembled British parliamentarians that it is liberty (which the Turk lacks) that is the 'nurse of all great wits':

> If it be desired to know the immediate cause of all this free writing and free speaking, there cannot be assigned a truer than your own mild and free and human government. It is the liberty, Lords and Commons, which your own valorous and happy counsels have purchased us, liberty which is the nurse of all great wits. This is that which hath rarefied and enlightened our spirits like the influence of heaven; this is that which hath enfranchised, enlarged, and lifted up our apprehensions degrees above themselves... We can grow ignorant again, brutish, formal and slavish, as ye found us; but you then must first become that which ye cannot be, oppressive, arbitrary, and tyrannous, as they were from whom ye have freed us.[68]

A factor that augmented the feeling of animosity and fuelled the fire of hatred towards Ottoman Turkey was the sectarian conflict within Christianity itself. The opposing (and sometimes warring) Christian sects charged one another with an implicit or explicit alliance with the Turks against Christendom. Sir Thomas More, for example, attacks Luther's teachings of non-resistance as a hindrance to Christian determination to withstand the Turk:

> And in this opinion [non-resistance] is Luther and his followers which, among their other heresies, hold for a plain conclusion, that it is not lawful to any Christian man to fight against the Turk... Though he come into Christendom with a great army and labour to destroy all. ... And if the Turk happen to come in, it is little doubt whose part they will take, and that Christian people be like to find none so cruel Turks as them. It is a gentle holiness to abstain for devotion from resisting the Turk, and in the meanwhile to rise up in routs and fight against Christian men, and destroy as that sect hath done, many a good religious house, spoiled, maimed...[69]

The Protestant Milton claims that it is the Pope who hinders the fight against the Turks: 'What by his [the Pope's] hindering the Westerne Princes from ayding them against the Sarazens, and Turkes, unlesse when they humour'd him...'[70]

Regardless of his claim that the Pope hindered the Christian fight against the Ottoman Empire, Milton was very much conscious of the benefits England could reap from trading with the Turks. In *A Declaration Against Spain* (1655), he says that neither the Pope nor the Spanish monarch has the right to 'prescribe us bounds of trade... inhibiting all Trade and commerce with Turks, Jews, and other infidels'.[71] Milton is here thinking in terms of British national interest. During the fourteenth and fifteenth centuries, England relied mostly on Venice for the execution of its trade with the Ottoman Empire. In 1553, trading privileges were first granted to Anthony Jenkinson by Sultan Suleyman I (r.1520–66), marking the beginning of official trading between England and Turkey. Jenkinson was given freedom to trade throughout the Ottoman Empire on a par with the French and the Venetians.[72] However, it was Queen Elizabeth herself who personally promoted relations with Turkey in the hope that those relations 'might prove a useful counterpoise to Spanish power in the Mediterranean'.[73] Two Englishmen, Sir Edward Osborne and Richard Staper, made steps to improve British trade with Turkey. After a stay of eighteen months, one of those agents 'secured from the Sultan a safe-conduct for Osborne's factor, William Harborne, allowing him free access to the Sultan's dominions'.[74] Harborne set out for Constantinople in 1575, and by his tireless efforts, letters were exchanged between Queen Elizabeth and Sultan Murad III (Amurath). An agreement regulating English trade with the Ottoman Empire was signed by the Sublime Porte in September 1581. As a result, the celebrated Levant Company (or 'Company of Turkey Merchants') was created. Previously, English merchants in the Levant had been trading under French protection.

In 1582 William Harborne was appointed ambassador at the Sultan's court. The expenses of the diplomatic mission were borne by the Levant Company, and Harborne served as both a diplomat and a merchant. Queen Elizabeth was interested in fostering those relations, and, on the accession of Sultan Mehmed III in 1595, she sent him a shipload of gifts to court Ottoman support against her Catholic enemies. For more than two centuries, the Levant Company (dissolved by Act of Parliament in 1825) contributed substantially to the promotion of commercial and political relations with the Ottoman Empire. Interestingly enough, English diplomatic officials in the Turkish territories were employees of this company (one of them was Edward Pococke). The traditional antagonistic attitude was thus tempered by growing political and commercial realities. Milton, as Secretary for Foreign Tongues, was very much in touch with the political situation and the interests of his own country when he objected to the papal law prohibiting trade with the Ottoman Empire.

Capitalising on the Venetians' loss of naval supremacy in the Mediterranean, England started to open commercial routes with Ottoman Turkey. Despite Francis Bacon's and Henry Marsh's calls for the renewal of Crusades against the Turkish threat, self-interest prevailed. The intensive commercial activities initiated between England and Turkey by Queen Elizabeth and Sultan Murad (1574–1595) made some Europeans suspect that the queen was planning to offer the Turk a safe port to help him establish a foothold in Western Europe. Queen Elizabeth was so enthusiastic about promoting those relations that she even ordered her fleet commanders, who had attacked Cadiz in 1595, to release Turkish slaves from captured Spanish ships. The officers were pleased, as Richard Hakluyt (1552–1616) reported, 'to apparel them, and to furnish them with money, and all other necessaries, and to bestow on them a bark and a pilot, to see them freely and safely conveid into Barbary'.[75]

British contacts with the Levantine and Mediterranean Muslims were strong, and Turks and Moors were to be found on English soil as traders, diplomats, and even as pirates. They were admired for their strange clothes, particularly their headgear, and stately manner of walking. They offered to the monotonous daily life of Londoners a taste of the exotic, the different, and the other. Interestingly, British ships and crews began to transport Muslim pilgrims to Mecca, relieving them of the notorious treatment of the Maltese pirates. Intimate knowledge of and acquaintance with Muslims gradually began to brush aside the old stereotypes perpetuated by travellers and writers.

As a result of these improved relations, more objective material about Ottoman Turkey began to appear. Sir Paul Rycault's book *The Present State of the Ottoman Empire, Containing the Maxims of the Turkish Politic, the Most Material Points of the Mohammedan Religion* (1668) shows a sympathetic approach based on actual knowledge of Turks. The demonising of Turks that was rife and derived from fantasy, fiction, and hearsay began steadily to give way to accounts about real men whom the Britons knew in daily life. That is probably why, to quote Nabil Matar, 'unlike Spain, France, Portugal, and Italy, England did not produce an anti-Muslim epic; Spenser's and Milton's epics make only few allusions to "Turks" or Mohometans'.[76]

There was a burgeoning Muslim community in Elizabethan London, and a thriving English community in Turkish lands. James Mather showed in his book *Pashas: Traders and Travellers in the Islamic World* that by the end of the seventeenth century, trade with Turkey accounted for one quarter of all England's overseas commercial activity, and that trade relations with Turks could be seen as a precursor to the centuries of British Empire ahead. Some Englishmen enjoyed their stay in Muslim lands so much that when Charles II sent Captain Hamilton to ransom Englishmen who had been enslaved on the Barbary Coast, some simply refused to return. They had converted to Islam and were 'partaking of the prosperous success of the Turks'.[77]

Not only Turkish Muslims, but also their co-religionists on the northern coast of the Mediterranean, were looking for English friendship and exulting in the English victories over the Spaniards. Abū Faris Abd al-Aziz al-Fishtali (1549–1641), who served as a scribe at the court of Mulay Ahmad al-Mansur, wrote a very interesting letter that shows how joyful the Maghribi people were at the catastrophic defeat of the Armada in 1588. The debacle was seen as a victory for Islam in its deadliest struggle against Spain. Al-Fishtali heaped praise on Queen Elizabeth and her Christian subjects who were able to crush the 'polytheistic' Spaniards:

> The enemy of religion, the infidel (may God increase his sorrow and weaken his hold), the tyrant... of Qishtala [Castile] who is today against Islam and who is the pillar of polytheism... and the one against whom both sword and destruction should, by religious duty, be wielded: he met his kind in the Sultana of the lands of Niglateera [England] whom God has turned, from among his kind, into an enemy to preoccupy him. Their enmity started after she and her people renounced the religion and law of the Christians, and left their denomination... Like the coming of the night, her sea ships repeatedly fell on his fleets until he began to suffer from her as from an incurable disease... so he decided to send his fleet against her lands, and to confront her with his armies on her own turf... he exhausted the near and far, until he had a formidable fleet... the fleet sailed to the lands of Niglateera... God sent a share wind... that broke up their formation and pushed them onto the enemy's lands bringing down their flags and banners. Niglateera saw an opportunity and seized it. [The English] fleet attacked the

strong fleet and brought upon it defeat... The sign
that shows that the time of conquest [of Alandalus]
is approaching, with God's will, and that the hour
and instance are at hand is the arrival, at this time, of
a messenger from the keeper of Constantinople who
is coming... bespeaking peace with us... perhaps...
the unity of Islam by this peace which is soon to be
announced between the two countries and confirmed
between the two kingdoms [the Ottoman Empire and
Morocco] will help to turn all attention, with God's
help, to fight the enemy of religion and to attack the
parties of atheistical polytheists until God fulfills for
him [al-Mansur] his promise in this dear matter, to
conquer the lands, God willing, far and near, and to
expel the nation of infidelity from its strongholds and
outposts, with God's help and might.[78]

Al-Fishtali viewed the English victory over the Spanish as
an opportunity to reconquer Spain and restore it to the fold
of Islam. He and his master al-Mansur apparently enter-
tained the idea that an alliance between Turkey, Morocco,
and England was possible, and that a new stage in the
international power struggle was in the making.

Other Christians who did not share the traditional
European prejudice towards the Ottoman Turks were
members of the Greek Orthodox church. The Greek
patriarch of Jerusalem viewed the Ottomans (as late as the
eighteenth century) as God's messengers sent to guard the
Orthodox faith:

See how clearly the Lord, boundless in mercy and all-
wise, had undertaken once more the unsullied holy

and Orthodox faith… He raised out of nothing this power empire of the Ottomans, in place of our Roman [Byzantine] Empire which had begun, in a certain way, to cause to deviate from the beliefs of the Orthodox faith… The all-mighty Lord, then, has placed over us this kingdom, 'for there is no power but of God,' so as to be to the people of the West a bridle, to us the people of the East a means of salvation. For this reason he puts into the hearts of the Sultans of these Ottomans an inclination to keep free the religious beliefs of our Orthodox faith and, as a work of supererogation, to protect them, even to the point of occasionally chastising Christians who deviate from their faith, that they have always before their eyes the fear of God.[79]

In its own time, the Ottoman Empire was a model of a pluralistic society. It even devised a system, called 'the millet', which served as a framework within which Jews, Christians, and other religious and ethnic minorities functioned. The Greek communities were allowed to maintain their forms of worship and their language for centuries after the fall of Constantinople. In the Balkans, the building of churches and the freedom of the clergy in shepherding their congregations were permitted, and national minorities enjoyed a happy coexistence with the Turks. It should be stated that the Turks' permitting 'liberty of conscience' was in keeping with the egalitarian spirit of Islam. According to Muslim law, followers of monotheistic faiths should not be obliged to change their creeds and only idolaters were not entitled to this privilege.

Although Milton, like most of the Europeans of his generation, held the idea that the Turks represented the prime enemy of Christendom, he never advocated their killing. In his definition of holy war (already quoted), he refers to 'Gower. 1.4. fol. 61. 72'. The reference is to *Confessio Amantis*.

> Amans, the lover, asks the confessor:
> I prei you tell me nay or yee
> To passe over the grete See
> To werre and sle the Sarazin,
> Is that the lawe?
> The answer was:
> Sone myn,
> To preche and soffre for the faith
> That have I herd the gospel seith
> But forto slee, that hiere I noght.[80]

Milton even, occasionally, had a good word to say about Turks. In *Of Reformation* he praises the 'Turkish and Jewish rigor against whoring and drinking'.[81] Milton was also aware of the plain fact that the Bible does not incite Christians to kill. In *Tenure of Kings and Magistrates*, he explicitly writes:

> Who knows not that there is a mutual bond of amity and brotherhood between man and man over all the world... Nor is it distance of place that makes enmity, but enmity that makes distance.
>
> He therefore that keeps peace with me, near or remote, of whatsoever nation, is to me as far as all civil and human offices an English man and a neighbor. But if an Englishman, forgetting all Laws, Human, civil, and religious, offend against life and liberty, to him

offended and to the Law in his behalf, though born in
the same womb, he is no better than a Turk, a Saracen,
a heathen.[82]

There is a tone of toleration and an emphasis on human
relations regardless of any racial or geographical differences.

A fair treatment of Muslims can be found in Thomas
Fuller's *The Holy Warre* (1639). He singles out the Muslim
virtue of toleration for praise: 'To give the Mahometans
their due, they are generally good fellows in this point
[toleration], and Christians among them may keep their
consciences if their tongues be fettered not to oppose the
doctrine of Mahomet.'[83]

Milton did not condone strife among men. For him,
even love of one's country is not a sufficient excuse for
'plundering and bloodshed and hatred'.[84] In *Paradise Lost*,
the voice of the narrator rises to castigate those who 'live
in hatred, enmity, and strife/Among themselves, and levy
cruel wars,/Wasting the Earth, each other to destroy' (2,
501–2). Refusing Satan's offers of glory, riches, and pomp,
Christ states that

> They err who count it glorious to subdue
> By Conquest far and wide to overrun
> Large countries, and in field great Battles win,
> Great Cities by assault: What do these Worthies,
> But rob and spoil, burn, slaughter, and enslave
> Peaceable Nations, neighboring or remote,
> Made those their Conquerors, who leave behind
> Nothing but ruin wheresoe'er they rove,
> And all the flourishing works of peace destroy...
>
> (*PR* 3, 71–80)

Even victory itself cannot be achieved without the help of God, and, therefore, causes should be true and just. Quoting Theodoret's *Church History*, Milton writes that 'victory is based not on strength or military experience, but on whether he who begins the war has God on his side.'

Milton's attitude towards the Turks of the Ottoman Empire is complex. Religiously, he is in line with the traditional Christian polemic writings. Commercially and politically, he is an English patriot, viewing the whole issue within the context of national interest and European power struggle. From a purely humanitarian standpoint, there are instances when Milton transcends all differences and barriers separating one nation from another. In so doing, he asserts world brotherhood, love, and peace, reflecting the true teachings of Jesus Christ and contributing to the restoration of a lost paradise. He indeed inherited the medieval attitude, but he also had his own, independent view.[85]

IV

Milton in Arabic

1. The Man and the Artist

The way Milton has been handled in Arabic is a story of misunderstanding, of indiscriminate and undocumented repetition of the ideas of other scholars, and of gross generalisation. Although most of what has been written is directed at the general reader, not at the specialist, nothing warrants the hasty judgments passed on one of England's foremost poets.

Maḥmud al-Khafīf wrote thirty-five short essays on Milton and his art in the weekly *Ar-Risālah* (*The Message*) between 25 February and 30 December 1946. Although he did not state his sources, a casual perusal of these essays reveals a strange mixture of different scholarly ideas. He first established Milton as a Puritan 'in heart and mind',[86] reminiscent of David Masson's *Life of John Milton*, a work on which Al-Khafīf depended. In another essay, he stated that Milton was not 'a whole-hearted Puritan because he was not a one party man'.[87] This opinion recalls that of Macaulay.[88] In a third essay, Al-Khafīf takes Milton to be a production of Puritanism and the Renaissance. Here he is indebted to Stopford Brooke and Mark Pattison (he refers to Pattison by name).[89] He also repeats the traditional conception of Milton as a rough, serious, and uncompromising man, advanced by such critics as Saintsbury, Lowell, and Sir Walter Raleigh. However, the idea of the grimly austere Milton is tempered by constant references to Milton as the revolutionary bard who sang 'the most beautiful songs of liberty, beauty, and imagination'. (This description appears as a motto in the beginning of each of the thirty-five essays of Al-Khafīf.)

In their appraisal of Milton's artistic achievement, many Arab commentators have repeated a myriad of critical assumptions that they have yoked together. The critics followed are Samuel Johnson, William Hazlitt, Macaulay, Saintsbury, Lowell, and Taine. Khalil At-Wāl published three essays on Milton's life, works, and style.[90] The 'ideas of Milton,' he said, 'are commonplace. He knows how to dress familiar notions in exalted verbal expressions. When all the stylistic paraphernalia is removed, his ideas become very uninspiring.'[91] Milton's style is characterised as 'artificial', and 'factitious', as in Hazlitt's lecture 'On Shakespeare and Milton' (1818). At-Wāl, following Hazlitt, says that 'Shakespeare is the poet of nature who writes poetry comfortably. Milton, although we respect him as a great poet, is artificial and burdensome. His meanings, as a whole, are familiar and common and his imaginative flights are offensive to the poetic instinct and the literary taste.'[92] At-Wāl also adds that 'Milton combines in his poetry the vehemence of emotions and the weightiness of reason. That is, to him poetry is an art and a philosophy. His style runs naturally and smoothly when the ideas are clear in his mind, but it becomes utterly burdensome when the ideas are not crystal clear. He was apparently interested in hunting for strange obsolete Latin words.'[93] The alleged artificiality of Milton's style and his use of Latinised words were singled out as his chief stylistic sins. Arab commentators on Milton treat these notions as established critical facts.

Al-Khafīf praised Milton's sonnets as 'the whispers and expressions of a great noble soul'.[94] To him, the sonnets show Milton's ability to express great things in a few words. Milton's special form of the sonnet is taken as a proof of his poetic independence as an artist and his courage as a man. The fact that he did not follow Elizabethan practice in form as well as in subject matter is stressed. The sonnets particularly praised are 8, 18, 19, and 23.

To almost all Arab commentators, the demarcation line between Milton the man and the artist is nonexistent. In his essay 'The Poet of Paradise: John Milton'[95] Ḥasan Al-Manfalūṭī, an Egyptian essayist, compares Milton's life to a play in three acts. 'The first act spans Milton's life from 1608–1639, a period of experience and experiment during which Milton decided to devote himself unreservedly to the cause of justice and truth.' The second act in the drama of Milton's life covers the period from 1640–60. During this period, Milton waged war against the prelates and Charles I in a prose 'unmatched by any other English writer'. The third act (1660–74) presents the catastrophe or the resolution of the play. Milton's 'despair' during this period is dominant and all-encompassing. As a result, 'he resorted to Providence and took refuge in the haven of poetry'. *Paradise Lost* is viewed as Milton's 'defence of Man and life before the court of God'. Milton's 'final' work is a tragedy; Samson is a symbol of Milton's life, since Samson, the defeated hero, is Milton himself amid his foes. The tragedy of *Samson Agonistes* also stands for the British people who lived in a state of servitude under Charles I. Milton hoped that the people would destroy the 'temple' as Samson did. The poet of *Paradise Lost* died with this hope. History has judged Milton as the only one who saw in the age of the blind.

Two essays written by another Egyptian essayist named Ahmad Khakī are both entitled 'John Milton and His Poetry in Light of Recent Psychological Research'.[96] According to Khakī, Milton's poetry is a good example of how personal problems are transferred into universal concern. To illustrate this thesis, he gives Milton's treatment of women in his works as an example:

> Milton's handling of the fair sex is paradoxical: some-times he speaks of them as shrines of virtue, other times he condemns them as devils. The reason is that Milton was a sexual maniac [sic] restrained by religious and ethical standards. You can even detect this conflict between religion and desire in his poetry. This inner clash is then transformed into a struggle between the forces of good and evil in this world.[97]

This 'psychological' reading of Milton recalls some of the charges heaped on Milton by Saurat and Liljegren. It is indeed a sad thing that the psychological interests of Khakī did not yield anything positive and decent with regard to one of the most noble-minded and honourable men in the history of English literature.

Luwīs Awād, former professor of English literature at the University of Cairo, claims that Milton's beliefs are identical with the teachings of Islam. He says:

> When we read *Paradise Lost*, we feel that Milton is a devout Muslim. This is reflected in his rejection of prel-ates and their mediation between God and His crea-tures. You also find Milton as a lover of life on earth [sic]. He interprets the Bible in practical and personal

ways. He advocates divorce and considers man superior to woman. He also hates the rituals of the church and the icons. He draws on the Old Testament, not the New Testament. For these reasons, I have already said that Milton was not a Christian, but rather a pious Muslim.[98]

Awād is certainly right in seeing a similarity between some of Milton's principles and those of an ordinary Muslim, especially those related to divorce and the superiority of men. Nevertheless, he calls Milton a Muslim on the grounds of correspondence of beliefs. He does not investigate the sources of Milton's ideas. The source of Milton's idea of divorce is Deuteronomy 24.1–2:

> When a man hath taken a wife and married her, and it come to pass that she shall find no favour in his eyes, because he hath found some uncleanness in her; then let him write a bill of divorcement, and give it in her hand, and send her out of his house.

The Law of Moses, permitting divorce in specific cases, was Milton's authority on the subject. Milton refers to Moses some seventy-eight times, and speaks of him as an author 'great beyond exception' and as the 'inspired law-giver'.[99] Milton himself states that he read Selden's *Hebrew Wife* on fornication as a cause for divorce.[100] Milton's own marital problems provided an added incentive for his upholding of divorce. Those who object to it, Milton says, resort to custom which 'hinders man's search for the truth and restrains the reasonable soul of man'.[101]

The idea of the superiority of man over woman is certainly emphasised by Milton in his works. In *Paradise*

Lost, Adam is described as the head and the guide:

> Not equal, as thir sex not equal seem'd:
> For contemplation hee and Valor form'd,
> For softness shee and sweet attractive Grace,
> Hee for God only, shee for God in him:
> His fair large front and Eye sublime declar'd
> Absolute rule; and Hyacinthine Locks
> Round from his parted forelock manly hung
> Clust'ring, but not beneath his shoulders broad:
> Shee as a veil down to the slender waist
> Her unadorned golden tresses wore
> Dishevell'd, but in wanton ringlets wav'd
> As the Vine curls her tendrils, which impli'd
> Subjection, but requir'd with gentle sway
> And by her yielded, by him best receiv'd,
> Yielded with coy submission, modest pride,
> And sweet reluctant amorous delay.
>
> (4, 296–312)

Adam is physically and intellectually superior to Eve. He has the right of absolute rule, and she the duty of obedience and subordination. However, if Adam's superiority gives him prominence, it also makes him more responsible. To the unfallen Eve, her husband's superiority is her glory and dignity:

> O thou for whom
> And from whom I was form'd flesh of thy flesh,
> And without whom am to no end, my Guide
> And Head, what thou hast said is just and right
>
> (4, 440–3)

This is Eve's answer after Adam tells her of the prohibited tree and of the pledge of their obedience to the Almighty (4, 41–439). This idea of a male ascendancy is not restricted to Islam. As Marjorie Nicolson aptly says:

> It would have been impossible for Milton to feel differently. Apart from the fact that this was basic teaching of Hebrew and Christian – indeed, of pagan – religion, and that of law, stemming from Roman Law, it was also a basic concept of the 'hierarchy' or 'order' of the universe, almost universally accepted in Milton's time… Differentiation of the sexes into 'higher' and 'lower' was inevitable in the nature of things. If his position gave Adam precedence in some ways, it also made his responsibilities heavier.[102]

Milton's hatred of prelatical mediation and disbelief in images and icons derive from the Old Testament and Protestantism. It would have been more helpful had Luwīs Awād explained Milton's concepts in the light of that poet's Hebraic and Protestant studies.

Another point of similarity between Milton's ideas and those of Muslims which, although not mentioned by Awād, might be misunderstood as an Islamic influence on Milton is the belief in polygamy. Milton writes in *The Christian Doctrine*:

> Either therefore polygamy is a true marriage or all children born in that state are spurious: which would include the whole race of Jacob, the twelve holy tribes chosen by God. But as such an assertion would be absurd in the extreme, not to say impious, as it is the

height of injustice, as well as an example of a most dangerous tendency in religion to account as sin what is not such in reality; it appears to me, that so far from the question respecting the lawfulness of polygamy being trivial, it is of the highest importance that it should be decided.

The Protestant reformers, 'challenged by the lust of temporal lords', suggested polygamy as a possible alternative. Those Protestant leaders who permitted polygamy were none other than Martin Luther, Philip Melanchthon and Martin Bucer. Milton's first entry on polygamy was made from Justin Martyr, whose authority on the subject of polygamy among the Jews 'is the famous Jewish rabbi Tarphon or Tryphon, as he is called by Justin. Rabbi Tarphon assures the scholars questioning him of the sanction of polygamy among the Jews from the earliest times.' Milton gives evidence from the Old and New Testaments in support of polygamy in *The Christian Doctrine*. In *The History of Britain*, he refers to the multiple wives of both Britons and Saxons.

Omar Farrūkh, former professor of philosophy at the Lebanese University, states that Milton was greatly influenced by the 'Qur'ānic account of Satan's disobedience of God's orders'. Farrūkh bases his assumption on Satan's portrait in *Paradise Lost* as 'an echo of what is said of the devil in the Qur'ān'.[103] To the best of my knowledge, there is no concrete evidence that Milton read the Qur'ān. Milton's depiction of Satan, the war in heaven, and the fall of the devil and his followers are derived from the Old and New Testaments, the books of the Apocrypha and Pseudepigrapha, Talmud and Targums, as well as from classical mythology.

2. Milton and Abū al-Alā al-Ma'arrī

A recurring critical assumption in writings on Milton is his alleged indebtedness to the works of Abū al-Alā al-Ma'arrī. One of the greatest Arab poets, Al-Ma'arrī (973–1057) was struck blind before the age of six. This early loss of sight left him with a sense of pessimism occasionally accompanied by fatalism. He was also weak in body. His literary reputation and philosophical leanings attracted the envy and enmity of a good number of influential people who accused him of heresy. Undoubtedly, his criticism of certain rulers and clergymen added to the list of his foes. As a person, Al-Ma'arrī was noted for his frankness and honesty. As an artist, he possessed a linguistic power unparalleled in the history of Arabic literature, using strange words and difficult expressions. His style is always referred to as 'artificial' and 'affected', as 'elevated' and 'eloquent'. He was known also for his great memory, intelligence, and analytic faculty. Al-Ma'arrī subjected everything to the light of reason. In religious matters, he apparently preferred good deeds to all forms of rituals and sectarian dogma.

Al-Ma'arrī's most famous work is *Risālatu-al-qhufrān* (*Epistle of Forgiveness*), composed in prose as an answer to his friend Ibn al-Qārih (972–1030). Ibn al-Qārih had attacked some Arab writers, consigning them to hell for bad deeds they had committed. Al-Ma'arrī wrote his *Epistle of Forgiveness*, an imaginary journey to the other world, to show that those writers could be in Paradise. The traveller and the speaker in the work is Ibn al-Qārih himself. Paradise is described as a place surpassing all human comprehension, of sensuous pleasures and bodily delights.

In Paradise, Ibn al-Qārih meets many poets from the pre-Islamic and the Islamic eras. He also sees Adam.

The majority of Arab critics and literary historians believe that Milton's *Paradise Lost* drew on the *Epistle of Forgiveness*. Other poems of Milton have also been compared with Al-Ma'arrī's works. In 1886, an unsigned article appeared in *Al-Muqtaṭāf* (*The Selection*) magazine under the title 'Abu al-Alā al-Ma'arrī and the English John Milton'.[104] The article is one in a series comparing prominent figures in Islamic history with counterparts in English history. It is preceded by an essay comparing Saladin with Richard the Lionheart, and followed by another comparing Ibn Khaldūn with Herbert Spencer. In the essay on Al-Ma'arrī and Milton, the anonymous writer compares Al-Ma'arrī's description of the reflection of stars in the water and Milton's description of the reflection of Eve's image in the pool (*PL* 4, 454–5). He also compares Milton's famous lines on blindness (*PL* 3, 23–7) with similar lines written by Al-Ma'arrī. Nevertheless, these corresponding 'ideas' and 'images' are not indicative of Al-Ma'arrī's influence on Milton. They are images and notions common to all humanity. The fact that both poets became blind explains the correspondence in their treatment of blindness and light/darkness imagery. As a matter of fact, the anonymous author does not say that Milton was influenced by the Arab poet. He is specific that 'examples of these poetic correspondences are also found in the works of other writers as well'.

In 1904, the Lebanese writer Suleyman al-Bustani translated Homer's *Iliad* into Arabic. In the introduction, he writes that 'in the prose epic [sic] of Al-Ma'arrī, diverse materials are assembled. This foreshadows some of the visions of the Italian poet, Dante, and the English poet, Milton.'[105] This remark only indicates a correspondence.

Jūrjī Zaydān, a Lebanese literary historian, added to this sense of correspondence an element of direct influence and borrowing. He says that Al-Ma'arrī

> imagined in his *Epistle of Forgiveness* a man ascending to Heaven and describing what he sees there. This is what Dante, the Italian Poet, did in his Divine Comedy and what Milton, the English poet, did in *Paradise Lost*. Al-Ma'arrī preceded both of them. It is not strange to say that they [Dante and Milton] took the idea of an imaginary journey from him.[106]

Zaydān bases his assumption on the fact that Al-Ma'arrī lived before Dante and Milton rather than on any scholarly investigation into the likelihood that either European author had read Al-Ma'arri.

Zaydān also advances the thesis that Dante should have known the works of Al-Ma'arrī as a result of the contact between the Muslims and the Crusaders, but he does not offer the slightest evidence. Zaydān simply states that Milton took the idea of an imaginary journey from Al-Ma'arrī.

In the introduction to his translation of Macaulay's *Essay on Milton*, the Egyptian writer, Muḥammad Badrān, points out that 'there are many similarities between Milton and the great Arab poet and philosopher Al-Ma'arrī. Both were poets, prose writers, and philosophers and both were blind. Milton's *Paradise Lost* is similar to Abū al-Alā's *Epistle of Forgiveness*.'[107]

Omar Farrūkh says:

I cannot prove that Milton imitated Abū al-Alā, but I can show some general correspondences between the two in the following aspects: (1) the courage in the human penetration of the veil separating this world from the other world; (2) the material physical punishment; (3) the portrait of Iblīs [Satan] in *Paradise Lost*, especially in the first two books, is not like the devil's portrait in Christianity.

Aysha Abd al-Rahmān, former professor of Arabic at Cairo University, rightly says in her published dissertation on Al-Ma'arrī that 'those who claim that Milton borrowed from Abū al-Alā should apply themselves to scholarly comparison and research. I do not think the treatment of the other world in the works of the two poets justifies the claim of borrowing.'[108]

For the sake of completeness, it is worth mentioning three other elements in the works of Milton and Dante where comparisons have been drawn with Arabic writings.

Firstly, the traveller's passage in the *Epistle of Forgiveness* is barred by Khaytaur (the chief of the genies). Approaching hell, Ibn al-Qārih first sees the garden of the genies who believed in Prophet Muḥammad's mission. Khaytaur, sitting at the mouth of a cave, discusses with the traveller poems attributed to the genies as well as the language spoken by them. The path of Ibn al-Qārih is again barred by a lion and a wolf. In *Paradise Lost*, Satan is met by Sin and Death at the gate of hell. They momentarily bar his way, but, recognising him, they let him pass. In Dante's *Divine Comedy*, the traveller's road to hell is likewise barred by a leopard, a lion, and a she-wolf.

Secondly, in the *Epistle of Forgiveness* the entrance to hell is described as a volcano whose crater shoots forth fires. In *Paradise Lost*, hell is portrayed as a volcanic region whose 'liquid fire' continually burns (1, 225–37, 670–4). In each work, hell is also depicted as a dark and deep abyss.

Lastly, Satan and his followers in *Paradise Lost* are not only punished by fires of hell, but also by an exposure to coldness (2, 620–628). The Bible makes no mention of any punishment of cold in hell. The Qur'ān, however, alludes to the punishment of cold in stating that believers in Paradise shall suffer neither from the heat nor from the cold, *zamharīr* (LXXVI, 31). The celebrated Muslim mystic Ibnu'l 'Arabi says that Iblīs is punished by an exposure to ice and cold wind; the reason is that the devil is made of fire, and, thus, he is tortured by an exposure to the contrary element. Milton's source here is Dante's *Divine Comedy*, where Satan is plunged in ice at the lowest pit in hell.

These similarities are of the kind that is common to all people. The *Epistle of Forgiveness* exercised no influence whatsoever on *Paradise Lost*, since Milton had not even heard of it. Indeed, nothing in Milton's writings shows knowledge of Arabic literature; the two works are so different that any correspondence would seem insignificant. The differences could briefly be summarised as follows.

The sources of Al-Ma'arrī's *Epistle of Forgiveness* are the Qur'ān (particularly the story of al-Mi'raj or the ascension of Prophet Muḥammad to heaven), the theological interpretation of hell and heaven in Islam, pre-Islamic poetry, and some legends and superstitions known at that time. The sources and analogues of Milton's *Paradise Lost* are numerous, ranging from Homer and Virgil to Spenser and Tasso (not to mention the Bible and Talmudic traditions).

The sources of Milton are Hebraic and European. There are no references or allusions in *Paradise Lost* that suggest Milton was acquainted with, or had a knowledge of, Arabic literary heritage.

Paradise in the *Epistle of Forgiveness* is delineated as a place of physical delight where all imaginable sorts of bodily pleasures are practised. There are beautiful maids, singers, and cup-bearers. The inhabitants of this place are all poets, writers, and linguists. Adam is there as an art critic, passing judgments on certain literary and linguistic problems. Groups of poets, critics, and grammarians engage in friendly debate. It is the vision of an unrestricted appetite. This sensuous place is totally different from Milton's Paradise. Milton's Garden of Eden is an idyllic abode full of all kinds of trees, flowers, and beautiful natural sights. It has nothing of the sensuousness of Al-Ma'arrī's Paradise. Adam and Eve are there, but in Paradise they are more like angels than ordinary people (4, 185–93). Milton's Eden is a place of innocence, purity, and simple love.

Whereas Al-Ma'arrī described Paradise in vivid detail, specifying all kinds of pleasures and desires, he was brief in his portrait of hell. In Islam, hell is a dark burning place, having seven gates (XXXIX, 71; XV, 43–4). Its concentric gates correspond to the type and degree of sin. At the lowest stage of hell, there is a tree called *zaqūm* that has heads of devils for fruits. Dante's Inferno is depicted in a manner highly reminiscent of the Islamic hell. There are three groups tortured in Al-Ma'arrī's hell: tyrants, including kings and 'crowned women', Iblīs (Satan), and some pre-Islamic poets. The torture here lacks the intensity of pain we find in Dante's *Divine Comedy* and Milton's *Paradise Lost*. Al-Ma'arrī resorted to the meetings of poets and their literary debates that occupy most of his description of hell. This hell is inferior to Milton's magnificent portrait of the infernal place. Milton's hell is terrible, dark, and remote. There are indeed traces of Virgil's description of Hades, but Milton's hell is more complex and more painful than that of Virgil. Milton conceived of hell as both a physical place where the devils are materialistically punished, and as an inner state (like Dante's Purgatory). Unlike heaven, hell is a place of contradiction, disorder, confusion, and 'vile antitheses'.

The depiction of Satan in the *Epistle of Forgiveness* occupies only a short paragraph. We are told that Ibn al-Qārih, the speaker, sees Iblīs beaten with iron rods. There is a short dialogue between the two, centring on some very obscene questions raised by the devil. Ibn al-Qārih curses Satan for leading many souls to hell. Satan asks about that traveller's occupation, and is told that he is a man of letters. Satan says sarcastically that this is a miserable occupation that is hardly enough to meet one's needs (not to mention family support). Al-Ma'arrī's Satan is impassive and inactive (similar to Dante's), whereas Milton's is energetic and active.

It is also evident that the idea of an imaginary journey to the other world is a universal theme. In Homer's *Odyssey* as well as in Virgil's *Aeneid*, the hero visits the world of the dead. Dante's *Divine Comedy* is also envisaged as a journey to the other world. If Milton had borrowed the idea at all, he would have taken it from Homer, Virgil, and Dante. Al-Ma'arrī's source of a journey to heaven is the story of Prophet Muḥammad's ascension (al-Mi'raj) in the Qur'ān. And while nearly all the figures mentioned by Al-Ma'arrī are human and historical, in *Paradise Lost* the characters are either supernatural, drawn from the Bible and from classical legend, or abstract (such as Sin and Death).

Although Satan and Adam are in both the two works, in Al-Ma'arrī's Paradise he figures as a literary critic. He is asked by the traveller about the authenticity of certain verses attributed to him. This minor and uninspiring character is markedly different from Milton's Adam (a central figure on whose behaviour and guidance of Eve the destiny of mankind rests).

The *Epistle of Forgiveness* is a poet's vision of a life of desires. It is a prose epistle written as a reply to another epistle sent by a friend. *Paradise Lost* is an epic which was Milton's life-long dream and ambition, and in which he has attempted to 'justify the ways of God to men'. Al-Ma'arrī is a language critic judging fellow poets. Milton is a poet-prophet pursuing 'things unattempted yet in Prose or Rhyme'. Neither in subject matter nor in technique or any other artistic device are the two works similar. We only do injustice to Milton's 'graver' subject to compare it with Al-Ma'arrī's world of flesh. Moreover, the *Epistle of Forgiveness* was not translated into any European language before the twentieth century. Parts of the *Epistle of Forgiveness* were first translated into English by Reynold A. Nicholson in *The Journal of the Royal Asiatic Society* (1900 and 1902). Since there is no evidence as to Milton's reading of Arabic, any assumption about him being influenced by Al-Ma'arrī's work is, ipso facto, incorrect.

Anīs al-Magdisī, a former professor of Arabic literature at the American University of Beirut, draws a parallel between Milton's *Lycidas*, written on the death of Edward King, and an elegy written by Al-Ma'arrī on the death of his friend Muḥammad al-Gūbuli.[109] In both poems, the dead person is a friend who died in his prime. Both express profound sorrow and question the meaning of life. Milton calls upon nature to weep for Lycidas, and Al-Ma'arrī asks the birds to participate in the mourning. Al-Ma'arrī ends his poems with a consolation that everything is going to die including the stars and earth itself. Milton ends his poem by asking the sad shepherds to stop weeping: 'For Lycidas your sorrow is not dead,/Sunk though he be beneath the wat'ry floor.' There are indeed similarities in two poems written on a friend's death. But, Al-Magdisī failed to read Milton's poem in the light of the conventions of the pastoral elegy. When he asks the shepherds to stop weeping or when he calls upon nature to take part in the mourning, Milton is following the traditions of Bion, Moschus, and Theocritus.

Al-Ma'arrī does not compare himself and his dead friend with shepherds. Al-Ma'arrī's poem is built on the *ubi sunt* theme of the fickleness of life and the uncertainty of the human condition. Al-Magdisī's comparison of the two poems is typical of the way Milton has been handled by Arab writers. The problem with accepting the views of most of these writers is their indiscriminate treatment of general human sentiments and visions in terms of correspondences, influences, and borrowings.

3. The Character of Satan

The cult of Satan, which was a product of the English Romantic imagination, has influenced the understanding of most Arab writers of the character of Satan in *Paradise Lost*. Satan has been viewed by the majority of Arab writers and critics as the hero of Milton's epic, as a brave figure, as an active and exemplary revolutionary, and has also been equated with Milton himself. These fallacies have led to erroneous interpretations of *Paradise Lost* as a poem centring on the character of the devil. Milton's subtle delineation of Satan in gradual transformation and his role as a narrator in the poem have not been taken into critical account when the character of Satan is discussed.

Ṣafā Khulūsī, former professor of Arabic at the University of Baghdad, considers Satan to be 'Milton himself, Milton the revolutionary who allied himself with Cromwell... Milton was defeated in his struggle here on earth and tried to make up for it in the heroism of Satan in heaven. He says through the Prince of Darkness what he dared not say in public. Milton even became a Prince of Darkness after he lost his eye-sight.'[110] Khulūsi believes that Milton 'wrapped Satan in the mantle of glory, greatness and majesty'. Thus he quotes Milton's lines:

> What though the field be lost?
> All is not lost; the unconquerable Will
> And study of revenge, immortal hate,
> And courage never to submit or yield:
> And what is else not to be overcome?
> That glory never shall his wrath or might
> Extort from me.
>
> (*PL* 1, 105–11)

to show that *Paradise Lost* is 'full of all meanings of heroism, a defense of Satan.' Khulūsī is probably not aware that the speaker is not Milton; it is Satan.[111]

The narrator in *Paradise Lost* offers a particular point of view and perspective from which the whole scheme of action in the poem can be seen. He is a commentator, an analyst, and a keen observer of the whole course of events, not a mere storyteller. It is his voice that guides the steps of the reader in his attempt to grasp the meaning of the work. This narrator takes the role of a negative commentator with regard to Satan's speeches. When God, Christ, or an unfallen angel speaks, the narrator hastens to confirm the utterance. Certainly, the main efforts of the narrator focus on neutralising the speeches of Satan. A.J. Waldock says:

> If one observes what is happening one sees that there is hardly any great speech of Satan that Milton is not at pains to correct, to damp down and neutralize. He will put some glorious thing in Satan's mouth, then, anxious about the effect of it, will pull us gently by the sleeve, saying (for this is what it amounts to): 'Do not be carried away by this fellow: he sounds splendid, but take my word for it...' We have in fact... two levels: the level of demonstration or exhibition, and the level of allegation or commentary; and again there is disagreement. What is conveyed on the one level is for a long part of the time not in accord with what is conveyed on the other. Milton's allegations clash with his demonstrations.[112]

Arnold Stein states that Milton 'sets up a dramatic conflict between the local context of the immediate utterance and the larger context of which the formal perspective is expression. This conflict marks, with a literal accuracy and precision that are dazzling, the tormented relationship between the external and the internal despair.'[113]

The narrator's point of view concerning the falsity of Satan's speeches is reinforced by Satan's own soliloquies. Those soliloquies (which reveal the devil at moments when he is frank with himself) show the huge gulf separating

Satan's actual desperate situation on the one hand and his bragging on the other.

Early in Book 1, for example, the narrator informs his readers that Satan's rebellion against heaven's king was really motivated by pride and ambition:

> His pride
> Had cast him out from Heav'n, with all his Host
> Of Rebel Angels, by whose aid aspiring
> To set himself in Glory above his Peers
> He trusted to have equall'd the most High,
> If he oppos'd.   (1, 36–41)

In his soliloquy in Book 4 of the poem, Satan 'confesses' that the fault was his, not God's. Pride and ambition, which the narrator had already singled out, are affirmed by Satan himself:

> Pride and worse Ambition threw me down
> Warring in Heav'n against Heav'n's matchless King:
> Ah wherefore! he deserv'd no such return
> From Me, whom he created what I was
> In that bright eminence, and with his good
> Upbraided none.   (4, 40–5)

The narrator's comment has thus been confirmed and supported by Satan's very words. Khulūsī's interpretation ignores the crucial role of the narrator in *Paradise Lost*.

The narrator always comments on and corrects the speeches of Satan, lest the audience get carried away and deceived by Satan's 'eloquent' words. The lines quoted by Khulūsī as a 'proof of Milton's defense of Satan' should be read in the light of the narrator's comment that immediately follows:

> So spake th' Apostate Angel, though in pain,
> Vaunting aloud tho' racked with deep despair.
>
> (1, 125–7)

All Satan's bragging about his 'unconquerable will' and 'courage never to submit or yield' cannot hide that deep despair the devil actually feels. Khulūsī also objects to C.S. Lewis's treatment of Satan as a fool and a desperate adventurer who generates our laughter. He says:

> Professor C. S. Lewis, in his *A Preface to Paradise Lost* claims that Satan is a ridiculous and silly character, removed from all meanings of heroism... [however] the secret of the greatness of Milton's Satan resides in the fusion of heroic virtues and evil elements which makes Satan a great tragic personality. Where did, then, Professor Lewis's idea of Satan's ridiculousness come from? It is certainly built on [an analysis] of his [Satan's] bragging and lies. However, these braggings and lies are not that decisive to justify Lewis's remark [sic] ... As for Satan's folly, it is of the heroic type, since heroism needs, sometimes, a certain measure of folly... Heroism does not reside in fighting when you are sure of success; on the contrary, it resides in continuing the fight as your hopes for victory diminish (regardless of the folly implied here.)[114]

Satan's folly and despair are thus treated as heroic signs, pointing to the resolve and courage of the devil!

Maḥmud al-Khafīf sounds a similar note when he considers *Paradise Lost* as 'the story of Iblīs [Satan] who rebelled against God. We wonder how the poet created a long and elevated poem on this very simple and familiar story.'[115]

Khulūsī and Al-Khafīf are repeating old ideas about Satan that go back as far as John Dryden. If Satan is viewed as a hero, Milton's attempt to 'justify the ways of God to men' will be rendered absurd. Indeed, in the first two books of *Paradise Lost*, Satan gives the deceptive impression of heroism, although an examination of his motivations, designs, and future plans reveals a sly, intriguing, and mean creature. Even in the first two books of Milton's epic, 'Satan hardly seems heroic… when one reads carefully; he lies, deceives himself and others, boasts without foundation, aggrandizes himself, sets up situations to promote himself like any conman of the daily tabloids.'[116] Satan's decision to take revenge on God by tempting the two innocent and helpless creatures he has created is utterly incompatible with his claims of being equal to God. It was Shelley's understanding of Milton's Satan that influenced the Arab writers. Shelley saw in Satan the eternal revolutionary fighting authority. He wrote:

Nothing can exceed the energy and magnificence of the character of Satan as expressed in *Paradise Lost*. It is a mistake to suppose that he could ever have been intended for the popular personification of evil. Implacable hate, patient cunning and a sleepless refinement of device to inflict the extremest anguish on an enemy, these things are evil; and, although venial in a slave, are not to be forgiven in a tyrant;

although redeemed by much that ennobles his defeat in one subdued, are marked by all that dishonours his conquest in the victor. Milton's Devil as a moral being is as far superior to his God, as one who perseveres in some purpose which he has conceived to be excellent in spite of adversity and torture, is to one who in the cold security of undoubted triumph inflicts the most horrible revenge upon his enemy, not from any mistaken notion of inducing him to repent of a perseverence in new torments. Milton has so far violated the popular creed (if this shall be judged to be a violation) as to have alleged no superiority of moral virtue to his God over his Devil.[117]

Nevertheless, Satan's heroism 'is a mere self-deception, and Milton's Satan deceives himself so well that he deceived Shelley into thinking him an inspiring symbol of revolt against political tyranny. For Milton, Satan was the archetypal tyrant. His reign in Hell is the express antitype of the reign of the Son of God by merit in Heaven.'[118]

Abas Maḥmud al-Aqqād, one of the outstanding twentieth century Arab writers, was influenced by the Shelleyan understanding of Milton's Satan. He wrote a whole book, entitled simply *Iblīs*, on the character of Satan. In the preface to this book, he says that he is writing the 'history of Lucifer in order to derive from it the historicity of human morality as embodied in life dualism, good versus evil'.[119] He then surveys the portraits of the devil in Egyptian, Indian, Mesopotamian, and Greek religions and cultures. This introductory background is followed by a study of Satan in the three monotheistic faiths (Judaism, Christianity, and Islam). Finally, he discusses poetic devils in Arabic literature, and Satan in French, German, and English literatures. The devil Milton portrays, Al-Aqqād says, 'is more important than the poetic Satans depicted by his predecessors and followers'. He adds that Milton drew the attention of his readers to Satan by making him the central figure and by giving him ample opportunity to explain the cause he is fighting for. Milton's concentration on the character of the devil, Al-Aqqād believes, betrays that poet's admiration of the Satanic. The reason for so doing is that Milton himself was a rebel who found in Satan's mutiny a chance to voice out his revolutionary arguments.' Satan, according to Al-Aqqād, stands for Charles I, Cromwell, and Milton simultaneously. It represents 'Charles I in what the poet thinks objectionable and mean, and Cromwell in boldness, bravery and dignity'. The devil is also similar to Milton in his devotion to freedom and emancipation from restrictive authority. 'The portrait of the devil thus varies from one place to another in the poem, but there is a fixed satanic image which does not change in the mind of the poet.'

Pre-Islamic poets believed that each poet had his own poetic devil or *shaytān*. Those genies were believed to have their own tribes and habitat (usually ruins, uninhabited deserts, brooks, wells, and bushes). They also have the power to take any form they like. The most important of the abodes of the genies are *Abgār* and *Wibār*. Whereas the English word genius is derived from genie, the Arab word *Abgari* (a genius) is derived from *Abgār*. There are numerous stories in Arabic literature relating encounters between humans (particularly poets) and genies (who are accomplished poets themselves).

Al-Aqqād wrote a poem entitled 'Tarjamatu Shaytan', i.e. 'A biography of a Devil'. The depiction of Satan in this interesting poem is markedly different from the standard portrayal of devils in Arabic literature.[120]

Satan in Islam is both proud and disobedient. In the Qur'ān, Satan is described as having both traits. He refuses to kneel to Adam when ordered to do so by God. Satan protests he is superior to Adam, since he was made of fire while Adam was made of clay. (See The Qur'ān, Al-Isrā, verses 61–5.) God then dismissed him. Satan asked that God grant him the power to lead humans (who are not true believers) astray, and that his punishment be deferred until the Day of Judgment. He was granted these two wishes. His first crime was to tempt Adam and Eve, coming to them as a serpent in disguise. Iblīs and his followers will be cast, at the end of time, into hell. The difference between Iblīs and al-Shaytān is that Iblīs retains his proper name when it is a question of his refusal to bow down before Adam, but when he is the tempter, he becomes at-Shaytān.

With the exception of Satan's description as proud in the Qur'ān, we do not come across any proud devils in Arabic literary heritage. Al-Aqqād summarises his poem as follows:

> In this poem there is a story of a devil who is fed up with the lives of devils, and, as a result, has decided to repent. Previously, he was ordered by the Creator to tempt people. He decided to repent and God accepted his repentance and allowed him to enter Paradise. However, Satan found Paradise as a place of slavery. He rebelled against God. God then changed him into a stone.

Al-Aqqād wrote the poem after he read many epics and legends of the West. It was first envisaged as a work that was to be called *The Memoirs of a Satan*. After he had finished writing the first chapter, he decided, by the end of the First World War, to give the idea up. The alternative was 'Tarjamatu Shaytan'.[121] There are stanzas, episodes, and numerous references in Al-Aqqād's poem which remind the reader of Milton's *Paradise Lost*. After staying a short period in Paradise, Satan bursts in indignation at what he calls 'the life of restriction' and prefers hell to heaven (165–70, 194–5). This recalls Satan's address to Abdiel in *Paradise Lost* (6, 165–70). In Al-Aqqād's poem, angels notice the horrible disfiguration on the face of Satan as he reaches Paradise. This reminds readers of the changes on Satan's visage when he first glimpses Eden (4, 114–28). Both poets emphasise Satan's pride, envy, and tyranny. In both works, Satan undergoes a metamorphosis. In Milton's *Paradise Lost* Satan begins as a Titan and ends as a snake. There is a difference, however. The transformation of Al-Aqqad's Satan into a stone comes as a result of an 'arbitrary' decision by God. The reader is even shocked to find an intelligent creature changed, without enough justification, into a stone. The change of Milton's Satan is an internal process which Satan himself has brought about.

Al-Aqqad's depiction of God's character in the poem is a rare example in the history of Arabic literature. He first orders Satan to tempt people and then accepts his repentance and welcomes him to heaven, only for Satan to renounce his new life there. God, in retribution, changes him into a stone; Satan has predicted that God will change him, and accepts this as preferable to life in heaven. Satan's dislike for God's orders to tempt people puts him in an interesting and peculiar position. Al-Aqqad's Satan is similar to Shelley's Prometheus. The reader has no choice but to sympathise with this Satan since he is presented as a friend of man. However, what appears to be nobility and bravery in Al-Aqqād's Satan is mere despair in Milton's. Al-Aqqād's misunderstanding of the devil in Milton is due, I think, to Shelley's *Defence of Poetry*. Al-Aqqād knew Shelley via Al-Mazinī's booklet entitled *Poetry: Its Goals and Medium* (1915). In that booklet, Al-Mazinī quotes from Shelley's *Defence of Poetry*.[122] In an interesting article the Egyptian critic Hamdī as-Sakūt shows that Al-Mazinī discusses what he reads with his friends, chief among whom is Al-Aqqād.[123]

Another poem by Al-Aqqād on the same subject is 'Sibāqul Shayatīn' (*Contest of Satans*). Iblīs decides to offer a prize to the devil who shows extraordinary skill in tempting and deceiving humans. Seven of Satan's followers compete to win it. They are the satans of pride, envy, despair, regret, love, sloth, and hypocrisy. The satan of hypocrisy emerged victorious in that contest. The hypocrite devil, true to his nature, abstained from taking it; but Satan, aware of his follower's falsehood, offered him the prize. Like Milton's Satan, the devils presented in Al-Aqqād's poem are dynamic, energetic, and active. Temptation of mankind is the central theme in *Paradise Lost* and in the *Contest of Satans* Al-Aqqād singles out hypocrisy as the most dangerous satanic quality. Milton's Satan (himself the very embodiment of hypocrisy) uses this trait as a successful tactic in the deception of his followers and of Eve. In other works of Al-Aqqād, comments on Milton's Satan show Shelleyan understanding. He says that 'Milton imagined his Satan in most instances as the vanquished for whose defeat we feel sorry'.[124]

The idea of an energetic Satan had captured the imagination of Arab poets. The Egyptian poet Abdul Rahmān

Shukrī, a close friend of Al-Aqqād, composed a prose work entitled *Hadithu Shaytan* (*A Satan's Talk*). In the introduction to this work, he says:

> Recently, more studies pertaining to human psychology have appeared. However, those studies are still modest, like a drop of water that might be followed by a deluge. In this book *A Satan's Talk*, there are skepticism, puzzlement, sarcasm, and psychological analysis, which, combined, may awaken the human spirit. In the chapter containing Iblis's advice, there is, beneath sarcasm, my intention which is to show the shortcomings of having stagnant and unenergetic characters. I made Satan advise such persons to give up such state [of inactivity].[125]

Satan here takes the role of a sarcastic critic. Most of his criticism falls on inactive people. 'I see,' Satan says, 'in mute animals traits lacking in humans. Dogs are more faithful and honest, horses are more loyal and loving. Mules are more patient and resolute, and monkeys are more intelligent and imitative.' There are indeed Swiftian undertones in this attack on human nature, which is considered inferior to that of brutes. Shukrī ends his *A Satan's Talk* with advice to humans not to forget the 'fact' that there is a bond linking all creatures on this earth. Shukrī prefers Satan to slothful and unenergetic humans, who lead uneventful and uninspiring lives devoid of colour, dreams, and hope. There is no available evidence of Shukrī's reading *Paradise Lost*; however the underlying idea in *A Satan's Talk* has Miltonic (as well as Swiftian, Blakeian, and Shelleyan) resonances.

The Iraqi poet Jamīl Sudqi Az-Zahāwī published in 1931 a long poem entitled *Thawreh fil Jahim* (*A Revolution in Hell*). In 433 lines, he expressed ideas and sentiments that run contrary to established Muslim beliefs. This led to bitter attacks and accusations by sheykhs leading Friday prayers. Describing his poem, Az-Zahāwī stated that he wrote the poem after he failed to wage a revolutionary war on Earth.[126] *A Revolution in Hell* is probably the most courageous poem in Arabic literature, and the one which bears the strongest similarities to Al-Ma'arrī's *Risālat-ul-ghufrān* and Milton's *Paradise Lost*.

The speaker in the poem imagines himself dead and visited in his grave by Nākir and Nakīr (the angels of death in Islam), who are presented as arrogant and insolent. With horrible snakes in their hands, they initiate a series of questions about the identity and beliefs of the dead man. In response to their questions, the dead man states that he was a poet who dedicated himself and his art to the cause of freedom, righteousness, and truth. Asked whether he committed sins, he replies by emphasising his independence; the only sin was his free independent stand, which had differentiated him from all other people. Questions about resurrection, doomsday, punishment, reward, and Muslim paradise and hell follow. The speaker states that he has undergone numerous changes and conversions. At present, he says: 'I don't know my final belief and stand.' When asked about genies, Gabriel, and good and fallen angels, he makes clear that he does not believe in whatever the human mind rejects. In answer to a question about his concept of Godhead, the speaker gives a highly equivocal reply, which indeed betrays his lack of orthodox Islamic faith. The two angels of death become very angry and indignant. Protesting that even in death expression of one's beliefs seems to be forbidden, the speaker requests them to leave him comfortable in his grave. Is it not better, he movingly asks, to inquire about my conscience, faithfulness to friends, loyalty to my country, and fight for human rights and dignity? He also expresses his dismay at not being asked about his poetry, which was used for fighting 'reactionary forces' in society. 'I should be asked,' the speaker tells those angels, 'whether I contributed anything to the betterment of my people and country.' The angels of death tell him: 'All you have just stated, old man, is despicable and ridiculous' (173). They order him to answer briefly and directly. Their final question is about the deity the speaker believes in. He answers: 'You are now my only god/I live and die by your own will' (190–1). The angels condemn him as a heretic who must be punished for his faithlessness and denial of God's existence. They beat him and pour burning tar on his head.

To punish the man further, they decide to take him to heaven and hell. His visit to heaven is in order to see what he has, as a result of his heresy, deprived himself of. The description of Paradise is reminiscent of Al-Ma'arrī's and Milton's. As soon as he approaches Paradise, he smells the fragrance of flowers. He is so intoxicated that, for a while, he thinks himself drunk. This brings to mind Milton's description of Satan's feelings when he drew close to the Garden of Eden (*PL* 4, 152–71). There are delicious fish, fowl, fruits, and vegetables. Rivers of honey, wine, and milk flow, and all kinds of precious stones lie scattered over the evergreen earth. The Ḥuris (maids of Paradise) are also there. The speaker tries to drink, but the waters are ordered to retreat from his reach. Like Milton's Satan he is made to feel the extent of his loss. However, Satanlike as well, he prefers his grave to Paradise.

The visit to hell is modelled after Al-Ma'arrī's. Thrown headlong into that burning volcanic pit, the speaker finds himself in the midst of snakes and scorpions, lions and tigers. The fires of hell are vividly described and the inhabitants are materialistically punished (as the case is with Milton's devils). He meets poets, scientists, and thinkers. There are Al-Ma'arrī, Al-Mutanabī, Omar al-Khayyam, Dante, Shakespeare, Newton, Spinoza, and Darwin. Socrates, Plato, Aristotle, Avicenna, and Averroes are also there. Interestingly, Milton is not mentioned. In addition to inventing some weapons, the inhabitants of the infernal place manufacture a machine to extinguish the hellish fires. Milton's devils, we should here recall, are also inventors of weapons (6, 571–80).

The final episode in Az-Zahāwī's poem deals with the revolution itself. A youth delivers a speech in which he reminds the inhabitants of hell of the injustice inflicted on them, of their miserable situation, and of the necessity of taking over heaven. That youth draws their attention to the fact that their numbers exceed those of their adversaries. Likewise, Milton stresses the great numbers of fallen devils (1, 630–4, 775–92). A frightening sound is then heard; oceanlike, the inhabitants of hell are in a tumult. Al-Ma'arrī has fuelled the fires of revolution by telling his fellow revolutionaries that while 'fools dwell in heavenly palaces' they are being tormented in hell. War then breaks out. Satan and Uzra'il (soul-taker in Islam), respectively, lead the inhabitants of hell and their adversaries. Two battle lines, one white and the other black, are formed. The weapons used are winds, tempests, thunder, thunderbolts, seas, mountains, and volcanoes. Milton mentions thunder and thunderbolts as heavenly weapons (1, 93–4; 3, 328; 2, 166). Faithful angels in Milton's *Paradise Lost* tear up hills and cast them on their foes. The heavenly throne, as a result, is shaken in Az-Zahāwī's poem and in Milton's epic. The difference is that in *Paradise Lost* this claim is mentioned as one of Satan's numerous lies (1, 104–5). Az-Zahāwī's *A Revolution in Hell* ends in the total victory of the inhabitants of hell and the taking over of heaven.

Az-Zahāwī's poem was hailed as a 'little epic',[127] having religious, political, and social dimensions. Parallels and similarities exist between it and *Paradise Lost*. Besides those already pointed out, the most obvious is the idea of fighting a war in the other world. However, whereas Milton made heaven itself the battlefield, Az-Zahāwī chose hell. Khulusī believes that Az-Zahāwī took the idea of a war in the other world from Raphael's account in Book 6 of *Paradise Lost*.[128] Az-Zahāwī was known for his wide knowledge of European literature. Tāhā Hussein says that Az-Zahāwī was the poet of reason, the Ma'arrī of his time; but he was also the Al-Ma'arrī who got in touch with Europe.[129] Az-Zahāwī himself mentions that nothing used to please him more than 'reading works in Arabic or Turkish translations'. He specifies the works of Hugo, Tolstoy, Alexander Thomas, and 'other works whose authors I forgot'.[130] We cannot be sure whether he read Milton or not in the light of the existing biographical evidence.[131] Nevertheless, he was a close friend of both Al-Aqqād and Al-Mazinī, both of whom knew Milton via Shelley.

4. Translations

Zakī Najīb Maḥmud, a respected Egyptian thinker, translated the first one hundred and fifty-five lines of *Paradise
Lost* into Arabic verse.[132] He tried to preserve some of
Milton's poetic qualities; the unrhymed verse echoes
Milton's blank style, and quaint words recreate his elevated
diction. His manipulation of certain words, images, and
references remind Arab readers of ancient Arab poetry and
the Qur'ān. 'Sinai' in Milton's 'the secret top/of Oreb, or
of Sinai' (1, 6–7) was translated as 'Tor Sinīn', exactly as
it is used in the Qur'ān. Milton's words 'God', the most
High, 'the Almighty power' were rendered by the Qur'ānic
'Al-Barī', and 'Al-ly yal-Azīm'.

However, Zakī Najīb Maḥmūd changed or omitted
references in the original that contradict Islamic beliefs.
Milton's 'One Greater Man' was translated as 'prophet'. In
Islam, Christ is not considered as the son of God, but as a
prophet sent by God to draw people to the path of righteousness. The phrase 'He with his Thunder' was substi-
tuted by 'God in His Anger'. The association of God and
thunder would remind Muslims of the idols of pre-Islamic
tribes. The translation is thus adapted to accommodate the
convictions of Muslim readers.

The translator also at times misunderstands Milton's
frame of reference, consequently producing a faulty translation. Milton's 'Thou from the first/Wast present, and
with mighty wings outspread/Dove-like; satst brooding
on the vast Abyss/and mad'st it pregnant' (1, 19–22) was
translated as 'You were witness to creation/You sat dove-
like with wings overspread/Contemplating the Abyss till
you overloaded it with thoughts and poetry.' Milton here is

referring to the second verse of Genesis: 'And the spirit of God moved upon the face of the water'. 'Mad'st it pregnant' refers to the act of creation. It has nothing to do with 'overloading it with thoughts and poetry'.

There are instances where the translator fails to grasp Milton's poetic technique and his artistic intentions. He translated 'this great Argument' as 'grand essay'. Milton's 'that to the height of this great Argument/I may assert Eternal Providence/And justify the ways of God to men' was translated as: 'Help me so that I may with this grand essay reach a certain degree where I can assert Eternal Wisdom and vindicate God's mercy toward men.' In *Paradise Lost*, 'argument' is used to mean the development and the subject of the poem as well as the justification of God's ways. Moreover, in his translation of Satan's speech to Beelzebub, the word 'God' is used for Satan's 'he' and 'him'. This translation does not take into account Milton's subtle technique in making Satan refer to God as simply 'he' and 'him', a technique that shows the elaborate process of self-deception.

Confusion can also result from the translator's use of 'Iblis' for 'Beelzebub', since Satan and Iblīs are used interchangeably in Arabic. Finally, on occasion, Maḥmūd is misled by Arabic classical literature into translating Milton as if he were an ancient Arab poet. Although he does not fully grasp Milton's references and technique, generally speaking, his translation is effective and conveys the sense in a literary manner.

Muḥammad Anānī, of the English Department at Cairo University, published his translation of the first two books of *Paradise Lost* in 1982.[133] Anani's translation, with an introduction and notes, was the first academic attempt in

the Arab world to translate and explain Milton's epic to
Arab readers. In the introduction, he writes that he based
his translation on the text of the poem in *The Poems of John
Milton*, ed. J. Carey and A. Fowler (London: Longman,
1968), and that for notes, he drew on Phyllis B. Tillyard's
notes to *Milton: Paradise Lost, Book I and II*, ed. E.M.W.
Tillyard (London: Harrap, 1956), and on John Broadbent's
Some Graver Subject: An Essay on 'Paradise Lost' (London,
1960), as well as on William Empson's *Milton's God*
(London, 1961).

Anānī published in 1984 what he called Part Two of his
translation, which comprises the third, the fourth, and the
sixth books. His 1982 translation of the first two books was
reissued in 2001, a year in which Part Three of his translation (comprising Books 7, 8, and 9) appeared. Translation
of Books 10, 11, and 12 was finished in 2002. Anānī saw
to it that his translation of the twelve books of *Paradise
Lost* was published in one volume, which came out in 2002.
It took Anānī twenty years to translate Milton's epic. In
the preface to this volume, he dwelt on Milton's original
plan to write a tragedy entitled *Adam Unparadised*, and
pointed out certain artistic characteristics that permeate
Milton's work. This preface is followed by a comprehensive and detailed introduction dealing with seventeenth
century background material, including Milton's life, and
his angelic and cosmic views. Anānī is indeed preoccupied with the question he states in the opening lines of his
introduction, namely: how did Milton manage to write a
masterpiece at a time that witnessed a decline in literary
production and critical assessment? The translator did not
answer the question satisfactorily. He resorted, instead, to
mentioning a series of factual details, implicitly stating that

great geniuses transcend the constraints of time and over-come any political, social, or filial limitations. Nevertheless, Anānī succeeded, in 175 pages of explanatory notes, in illuminating and adequately clarifying Milton's biblical, mythological, and thematic references and connotations. His explanatory notes are also replete with translated quotations from the critical studies of eminent Miltonic scholars, which shed further light on important allusions and references in *Paradise Lost*.

Anānī must be commended for his excellent translation. The fact that he is an academician specialising in English literature is behind his precise translation and adequate knowledge of the details of Milton's epic. Like Zakī N. Maḥmud, he uses Qur'ānic terminology to render Milton's biblical references (1, 3 305–7, 125, 33 339). Anānī's success in retaining the poetic magnificence of Milton's similes and his mastery of the intricacies of the Arabic language are noteworthy. The result is an Arabic translation that matches the sublimity and splendour of the original English text.

The Egyptian journalist Abd al-Hamīd Hamdī trans-lated Milton's 'On Shakespeare', 'On Time', 'Sonnet: How soon hath Time', 'Sonnet XIX: When I Consider', 'Sonnet XXIII: Methought I Saw', and the first stanza of 'On the Death of a Fair Infant Dying of a Cough'.[134] These transla-tions are pedestrian prose renderings.

'Sonnet XIX: When I Consider' was translated under the title 'Milton in Rebellion'. This is misleading, since the poem ends in a note of acceptance, patience, and quiet. Another misconception is his translation of 'talent' in 'And that one Talent which is Death to Hide' as simply 'sense', meaning, 'sense of seeing'. Although this was at the back of Milton's mind, what was meant is more apt to be 'the poetic gift'. Milton had in mind the parable of the 'wicked and slothful servant' who neglects his lord's talent, hiding it under a bushel (Matt. 25:26). The translator adds and deletes lines at will. The first two lines of his translation of 'Methought I Saw' are not in Milton's poem, and he does not translate 5–8. His translation is a paraphrase of the general idea of the poem. Hamdī's translation of 'On Time' is probably his best. He retained the main metaphor of time versus eternity and most of Milton's images. However, in his translation of 'How Soon Hath Time', he failed to recreate Milton's sentiments in Arabic. He resorted to preaching, addressing time as treacherous, fickle, and unjust.

Ṭāhā Abd al Hamīd al-Wakīl's prose translations of sonnets VIII and XIX are superior to the verse renderings of Abd al-Hamīd Hamdī. Al-Wakīl grasped the meanings in the two sonnets and succeeded in preserving the eloquence of Milton's poetic style. He translated 'talent' in Sonnet XIX as 'poetic genius'. The sonnets were faithfully translated without additions or deletions. We also sense Milton's spirit in these translations, particularly his glorification of the art of poetry in VIII.

Ṣafā Khulūsī translated 'Lycidas', 'The Piedmont Sonnet' and lines 53–74 of 'L'Allegro'.[135] Khulūsī is better as a translator than he is as a critic. His prose translation of 'Lycidas' is sound and pleasing because he has a good command of English and Arabic. He understands the pastoral conventions and manages to retain the rural atmosphere of the poem. The only shortcoming is his translation of lines 27–31 as 'we together heard the imprisoned sound of violent winds, which was a prelude to wetting our sheep in the fresh dews of night'. Khulūsī thus failed to convey the time sequence Milton had in mind. 'The opening eyelids of the morn' followed by 'the heat of the noon', 'The fresh dews of night', and 'the bright Star that rose at Ev'ning' were relevant to student life at Cambridge where Milton and Edward King studied. 'At Cambridge, students began the day at five o'clock with morning prayers and services, went to breakfast at six, and to classes at seven. They were together in the morning, at high noon ('what time the Gray-fly winds her sultry horn'), throughout the afternoon and into the evening, when Hesperus, the evening star rose.[136]

Khulūsī translated the 'Piedmont sonnet' as an example of what he called 'revenge poetry in English literature'. The sonnet is not a revenge poem. It is rather a prayer or an invocation similar to what one can find in Revelation 6:9–10: 'The souls of them that were slain for the word of God… cried with a loud voice, saying, How long, O Lord, holy and true, doest thou not judge and revenge our blood.' Khulūsī translated the word 'cold' in 'whose bones/Lie scatter'd on the Alpine mountains cold' as an adjective qualifying bones, whereas it qualifies 'mountains' in the poem. His translation of 'L'Allegro' 53–74 is precise and poetic.

To the translator, these lines 'show a difference between the treatment of external nature in English and Arabic poetry', which is that 'the Arab poets do not describe nature for its own sake as Milton does. They usually link nature with female beauty.'[137]

A Postscript

It is legitimate to ask: what was it in the Arab world that brought about this great interest in John Milton's writings?

The interest of the majority of Arab critics and commentators resides in what they perceived to be Milton's revolutionary spirit, which championed the cause of freedom and fought indefatigably all forms of religious and political attempts to enslave individuals, institutions, or nations. Man's 'first disobedience' and Milton's attempts to 'justify the ways of God to men' are either ignored or very lightly touched upon. The Milton they celebrate, praise, and glorify is the one who justified Man's refusal of servitude and despotism. All the Arabic writings pertaining to Milton and his works discussed in this book are shot through with a mantra which hails him as the 'bard who sang the most beautiful songs of liberty', and spent his life defending Man's right to be free. The puritan Milton was thus presented as a freedom fighter who never lost hope that the British people would ultimately destroy the edifice of tyranny, and usher in a new dawn for themselves and for the rest of mankind. This is why the Iraqi Ṣafā Khulūsī maintains that the devil in Milton's 'graver subject' is no other than 'Milton the revolutionary who allied himself with Oliver Cromwell'. To Khulūsī and his like, Milton said through Satan 'what he dared not say in public', and made *Paradise Lost* in effect 'a defense of that devil's mutiny'. Indeed, the notion of the prince of darkness as a new Prometheus fighting for human rights has captured the imagination of Arab writers and critics.

This understanding on the part of Arab essayists and men of letters is due to the fact that they lived in a milieu in which the Arab elite were steadily absorbing the influence of Western civilisation and culture to which they were exposed when Napoleon conquered Egypt in 1798, and started disseminating the ideals of the French Revolution. The Egyptian Rifa'a al-Tahṭawi (1801–73) regarded modern European culture as a panacea for all the ills of Egypt. Al-Tahṭawi, who was sent in 1826 by Muḥammad Ali to study in Paris, was intoxicated by the rational views of the European Enlightenment. Upon his return to his native country, Egypt, he was made a director of the newly-established Bureau of Translation. He began in his post at this bureau by actively encouraging works of translation in all fields of human activity. To him and his fellow intellectuals, efforts had to be geared towards achieving a total renaissance in Egypt based on the European model.

This call for modernisation was given a new impetus by a group of writers, mostly Lebanese and Syrian, who settled in Cairo during the 1870s. Most of them were Christians educated in the French and American missionary schools, who had thus had access to Western culture. As Karen Armstrong writes: 'Their influence was enormous. In particular, these Christian Arabs were keen that the Muslim states should become secular, and insisted that science alone and not religion was the basis of civilisation. Like Tahṭ awi, they were in love with the West, and communicated this enthusiasm to the people of Egypt.'[138] Despite opposition from certain religious and conservative groups, the march towards modernity had begun. Consequently, translations of philosophic, scientific, and literary works had gone unabated. This trend that had started in the middle of the nineteenth century continued into the early part of the twentieth century, the period of the awakening of the Arab masses who had just emerged from four centuries of Turkish domination. With the advent of the twentieth century, ideas of democracy, individualism, and equality began to penetrate deep into the very fabric of Arab societies in Egypt, Iraq, and greater Syria.

A number of courageous individuals who studied mostly in France were calling for changes in all spheres of life. Led by the formidable Ṭāhā Ḥussein (1889–1973), they went as far as calling for the separation of religion and state. To convey his ideas, Ḥussein followed a methodology based on a comparison between the status of the Egyptian society, to which he belonged, and French society, where he had studied. When he became a minister of education, he immediately started to put his ideas of reform into effect. Like John Milton, he believed that the human self, regardless of race or creed, is built on knowledge, and that one's country is built by free individuals.

It is indeed noteworthy to find that most of those who commented on Milton and highly praised him were Egyptian contemporaries of Ḥussein's. Many of them were his friends, disciples, or admirers. Their translations and critical commentaries on Milton's works were published in the thirties, forties, or fifties, the heydays of Ḥussein and other reformers. Their interest in Milton resides not in his artistic designs or literary skill, but rather in his advocacy of freedom and denunciation of tyranny. The works of Milton touched a sensitive chord in the Arab psyche. Suppressed for centuries by brutal regimes, and subjected to all kinds of indignities and injustices, the Arabs did not have the luxury of appreciating art for its own sake. They simply upheld the notion that any writer is a committed and responsible individual who has a duty to fulfil towards his fellow citizens. To them, the demarcation line between fiction and nonfiction is nonexistent, and because of the prevailing political and social scene, they believed that a poet or a writer should be a legislator, a politician, and even a reformer. And, despite their hasty critical judgments and lack of grasp of basic literary tenets, those Arab commentators on Milton and his works deserve our admiration and respect because of their sincerity and their appreciation of basic human values and rights for which Milton stood so strongly.

Bibliography of writings about Milton in Arabic

(1) Criticism

Abd al-Rahmān, Ayshā, *Al-ghufrān* (Cairo: Dār Al-Mā'arif, 1945), pp. 92–102.

'Abū al-Alā Al-Ma'arrī and the English John Milton', *Al-Muqtaṭāf*, May 1886, pp. 440–56.

Al-Aqqād, Abas Maḥmūd, *Iblīs* (*Satan*) (Beirut: Dār al-Kitāb al Arabi, 1969), pp. 201–3.

Al-Bustani, Suleyman (trans.), *Ilyadhat Homar* (*Homer's Iliad*) (Beirut, 1904), p. 3.

Al-Khafīf, Maḥmūd, 'Milton': 25 short essays in *Ar-Risālah*, 25 February–30 December 1946.

Al-Manfalūtī, Hasan, 'Sha'ir al-jennah: John Milton' ('The poet of Paradise: John Milton') in *Ath-Thaqāfah*, 27 April 1948, pp. 17–19.

Al-Magdisī, Anīs, 'Merthiymyatan liftīgadi sadīq' ('Two Elegies on a Friend's Loss') in *Al-Arabi*, September 1967, pp. 52–8.

As-Sakūt, Hamdī, 'Ash-Shaytān: Al-Aqqād and Milton', *Fusūl*, July 1981, pp. 163–72.

At-Wāl, Khalil, 'John Milton' in *Ar-Risālah*, 25 October, 1 November, 8 November 1937, pp. 1741–3, 1784–6, 1824–6.

Awād, Luwīs, 'Al-adab al-Inglīzī adab 'ālāmī' ('English Literature is an International Literature') in *Al-Hilal*, 1 December 1967, pp. 219–22.

Badrān, Muḥammad (trans.), *Macaulay's Essay on Milton* (Cairo: Al-Khuniji Library, 1946), p. 1.

Farrūkh, Omar, *Hakīm al-Ma'arrah* (*The Sage of al-Ma'arrah*). (1944; rpt. Beirut: Al-Kashshāf, 1948), pp. 126–8.

Khakī, Ahmed, 'John Milton and his Poetry in Light of Recent Psychological Research' in *Ath-Thaqāfah*, 14 and 21 November 1939, pp. 16–18.

Khulūsī, Ṣafā, *Dirāsāt fil adab al-muqāran wal madhahib aladdabiyyeh* (*Studies in Comparative Literature and Literary Schools*) (Baghdad: Al-Rabitah, 1957), pp. 94–103.

Zaydān, Jurjī, *Tarīkh al-ādab al-Arabiyyeh* (*History of Arabic Literatures*) (vol. 2, Cairo: Al-Hilal, 1902), p. 226.

(2) Translations

Bibliography: See Abdul-Hai, Muḥammad, 'A Bibliography of Arabic Translations of English and American Poetry (1830–1970)' in *Journal of Arabic Literature* 7 (1976), p. 137.

Al-Wakīl, Tāhā Abd al-Hāmīd in *As-Siyasah al-Usbu'iyyah*, 21 June 1930, p. 6 (translations of sonnets VIII and XIX).

Anānī, Muḥammad, *Al-firdaws al-mafqūd: Malhamet al-Shā'ir al-Inglīzī John Milton* (*Paradise Lost: The Epic of the English Poet John Milton*) (vol. 1, Cairo: 1982). A translation with an introduction and notes, of Books 1 and 2 of *Paradise Lost*.

Anānī, Muḥammad, *Al-firdaws al-mafqūd*, 2002. A translation of the twelve books of *Paradise Lost*.

Hamdī, Abd al-Hamīd (trans.) 'On Time', 'Sonnet VIII', 'Sonnet XIV', 'Sonnet XXIII', and the first stanza of 'On the Death of a Fair Infant Dying of a Cough' in *As-Siyaseh al-Usbu'iyyah*, 11 June 1930, p. 24.

Khulūsī, Ṣafā (trans.), Translations of 'Lycidas', the 'Piedmont Sonnet', and lines 53–74 of 'L'Allegro' in *Dirāsāt fil adab al-muqāran wal madhahib aladdabiyyeh* (*Studies in Comparative Literature and Literary Schools*) (Baghdad: Al-Rabitah, 1957), pp. 118–25, 175–8, 148–9.

Mahmūd, Zakī Najīb (trans.) A translation of the first 150 lines of *Paradise Lost*, Book 1 in 'Min al-firdaws al-mafqūd' ('From *Paradise Lost*') in *Ar-Risālah*, 10 January 1937, pp. 778–80.

Bibliography of
Books and Articles Consulted

Abbūd, Marōn, *Abu al-Ala-al-Ma'arrī: zawba'tu al-dehir* (*Abu al-Ala-al-Ma'arrī: The Tempest of Time*) (3rd ed. Beirut: Dar Marōn Abbūd, 1970).

Abd Al-Rahmān, Ayshā, *Al-ghufrān* (Cairo: Dār Al-Ma'ārif, 1954).

Ackerman, Rudolph, *History of the University of Cambridge* (2 vols., London, 1815).

Adams, Robert M., *Ikon: John Milton and his Modern Critics* (Ithaca: Cornell University Press, 1955).

Addison, J.T., *The Christian Approach to Moslems* (New York: Columbia University Press, 1942).

Ahmed, Sami S., *Early Ideas of Evil and Devil* (Baghdad: Al-Jammia Press, 1970).

Al-Ahwānī, Abdul-Azīz, *Az-zajal fil Andalus* (*Az-zajal in Andalusia*) (Cairo, 1957).

Al-Aqqād, Abas Mahmūd, *Majmu'āt al-amāl al-kāmilah* (*Complete Works*) vol. 12 (Beirut, 1979).

—— *Dīwān al-Aqqād* (*Al-Aqqād's Collected Poems*) (Aswan, 1967).

Al-Ma'alūf, Shafīq, *Abgār* (San Paulo: Publications of al-usba al-andalusyyah, 1949).

Al-Māzinī, Ibrahim, *Abdul-Qadir: Al-Shi'ar: ghayatuhu wa wasa'luhu* (*Poetry: Its Functions and Medium*) (Cairo, 1915).

Ar-Rashūdi, Abdul-Hamīd (ed.), *Al-Zahāwī: dirāsāt wa nusus* (*Az-Zahawi: Studies and Texts*) (Beirut, 1966).

Az-Zarkli, Khayrud-Dīn, *Al-a'Alam* (*Outstanding Figures*) (rpt., Beirut: Dar al-'Ilm li al-Mayaleen, 1981).

Arberry, Arthur J., *The Cambridge School of Arabic* (Cambridge: Cambridge University Press, 1948).

—— *Oriental Essays: Portraits of Seven Scholars* (New York: Macmillan, 1960).

—— (trans.) *The Koran Interpreted* (2 vols., 1955; rpt. London: Unwin Brothers, 1963).

Armstrong, Karen, *The Battle for God: Fundamentalism in Judaism, Christianity and Islam* (London: Harper Perennial, 2004).

Arthos, John, *Milton and the Italian Cities* (New York: Barnes and Noble, 1968).

Atkinson, Thomas D., *Cambridge Described and Illustrated* (London, 1897).

Barker, Arthur, *Milton and the Puritan Dilemma* (Toronto: University of Toronto Press, 1942).

Benham, Allen R., 'Things Unattempted Yet in Prose or Rime' in *Modern Language Quarterly* 14 (1953), pp. 341–7.

Blochet, E., *Les Sources Orientales de la Divine Comédie* (Paris, 1901).

Boswell, J.C., *Milton's Library: A Catalogue of the Remains of John Milton's Library and Ancillary Readings* (New York: Garland Publishing Inc., 1975).

Bredvold, Louis, 'Milton and Bodin's Heptaplomeres' in *Studies in Philology* 21 (1924), pp. 399–402.

Broadbent, J.B., *Some Graver Subject: An Essay on Paradise Lost* (New York: Barnes and Noble, 1960).

Browne, E.G., *A Catalogue of the Persian Manuscripts in the Library of the University of Cambridge* (Cambridge, 1898).

Burckhardt, Titus, *Moorish Culture in Spain*, trans. Alisa Jaffa (New York: McGraw Hill, 1972).

Bush, Douglas, *Paradise Lost in Our Time: Some Comments* (Toronto: University of Toronto Press, 1945).

Campbell, Gordon, and Collins, Roger, 'Milton's Almansor' in *Milton Quarterly* 17 (October 1983), pp. 81–3.

Cantarino, Vincent, 'Dante and Islam: History and Analysis of a Controversy' in *Dante Symposium* (Chapel Hill: University of North Carolina Press, 1965), pp. 175–92.

Cash, W. Wilson, *Christendom and Islam: Their Contacts and Cultures Down the Centuries* (New York and London: Harper and Brothers Publishers, 1937).

Cawley, Robert, *Milton and the Literature of Travel* (Princeton: Princeton University Press, 1951).

Chaytor, H.T., *The Troubadours* (1912; rpt. Kennikat Press, 1970).

Chew, Samuel, *The Crescent and the Rose: Islam and England during the Renaissance* (New York: Oxford University Press, 1937).

Christopher, Georgia B., *Milton and the Science of Saints* (Princeton: Princeton University Press, 1982).

Cirillo, Albert, 'Time, Light, and the Phoenix: The Design of Samson Agonistes' in *Calm of Mind: Tercentenary Essays on Paradise Regained and Samson Agonistes in Honor of S. Diekhoff* (Cleveland and London, 1972), pp. 209–33.

Clark, Donald, *Milton at St. Paul's School* (New York: Columbia University Press, 1948).

Cooper, Lane, 'The Abyssinian Paradise in Coleridge and Milton' in *Modern Philology* 3 (1906), pp. 327–32.

Costello, William, *The Scholastic Curriculum at Early Seventeenth Century Cambridge* (Cambridge, Mass.: Harvard University Press, 1958).

Cross, Tom Peete, and Nitze, William A., *Lancelot and Guinevere: A Study on the Origins of Courtly Love* (Chicago: University of Chicago Press, 1930).

Crossman, Robert, *Reading Paradise Lost* (Bloomington: Indiana University Press, 1980).

Cullen, Patrick, *Infernal Triad: The Flesh, the World, and the Devil in Spenser and Milton* (Princeton: Princeton University Press, 1975).

Daniel, Norman, *Islam and the West: The Making of an Image* (1960; rpt. Edinburgh: Edinburgh University Press, 1980).

Dannenfeldt, Karl H., 'The Renaissance Humanists and the Knowledge of Arabic' in *Studies in the Renaissance* 2 (1955), pp. 96–117.

Darbishire, Helen, *The Early Lives of Milton* (London: Constable, 1932).

Diekhoff, John, *Milton's Paradise Lost: A Commentary on the Argument* (New York: The Humanities Press, 1958).

—— (ed.), *Milton on Himself: Milton's Utterances Upon Himself and his Works* (New York: Oxford University Press, 1939).

Dictionary of National Biography, eds. Leslie Stephen and Sidney Lee (21 vols., London: Oxford University Press, 1921–2).

Dorman, Harry Gaylord Jr., *Toward Understanding Islam: Contemporary Apologetics of Islam and Missionary Policy* (New York: Teachers' College, Columbia University, 1948).

Draper, J.W., 'Milton's Ormuz' in *Modern Language Review* 20 (1925), pp. 323–7.

Dunlop, D.M., *Arab Civilization to A.D. 1500* (London and Beirut: Longman and Librairie du Liban, 1971).

Farrūkh, Omar, *Hakim Al-Ma'arrah* (*The Sage of al-Ma'arrah*) (1944; rpt. Beirut: Al-Kashshāf, 1948).

Ferry, Ann D., *Milton's Epic Voice* (Cambridge: Harvard University Press, 1963).

Fish, Stanley, *Surprised by Sin: The Reader in Paradise Lost* (New York: St. Martin's Press, 1967).

Fitter, Christopher, 'Native Soil: The Rhetoric of Exile Lament and Exile Consolation in Paradise Lost' in *Milton Studies* 20, ed. J.D. Simmonds (Pittsburgh: University of Pittsburgh Press, 1984), pp. 147–204.

Fletcher, Harris F., *The Intellectual Development of John Milton* vol. 2 (Urbana: University of Illinois Press, 1961).

French, J. Milton, *The Life Records of John Milton* (6 vols., New Brunswick: Rutgers University Press, 1949).

Fry, Edward, 'John Selden' in *Table Talk of John Selden*. ed. Frederick Pollock (London, 1927), pp. 171–4.

Frye, Northrop, *The Return of Eden: Five Essays on Milton's Epics* (1965; rpt. Toronto and Buffalo: University of Toronto Press, 1975).

Frye, Roland M., *Milton's Imagery and the Visual Arts: Iconographic Tradition in the Epic Poems* (Princeton: Princeton University Press, 1978).

Fuller, Elizabeth Ely, *Milton's Kinesthetic Vision in Paradise Lost* (Cranbury: Associated University Presses, 1983).

Galbraith, V.H., *Roger of Wendover and Matthew Paris* (Glasgow, 1944).

Gardner, Helen, *A Reading of Paradise Lost* (Oxford: The Clarendon Press, 1965).

Gibb, Hamilton A.R., *Arabic Literature* (2nd ed., Oxford, The Clarendon Press, 1963).

—— *Mohammedanism: An Historical Survey* (Oxford: 1949).

Giffin, Lois Anita, *Theory of Profane Love Among the Arabs: The Development of the Genre* (New York: New York University Press, 1971).

Gilbert, Allen H., *On the Composition Of Paradise Lost* (Chapel Hill: University of North Carolina Press, 1947).

—— *A Geographical Dictionary of Milton* (New Haven: Yale University Press, 1919).

Grave, William, *Ideas in Milton* (Notre Dame, Indiana: University of Notre Dame Press, 1968).

Gray, Arthur, *Cambridge University: An Episodical History* (Boston and New York: Houghton, Mifflin Company, 1927).

Greene, Thomas, *The Descent from Heaven* (New Haven: Yale University Press, 1963).

Grierson, Herbert, *Cross Currents in English Literature of the Seventeenth Century* (London, 1929).

Groom, Nigel, *Frankincense and Myrrh: A Study of the Arabian Incense Trade* (London: Longman, 1981).

Hagin, Peter, *The Epic Hero and the Decline of Heroic Poetry: A Study of the Neoclassical English Epic with Special Reference to Milton's Paradise Lost* (Bern: Francke, 1964).

Haller, William, *The Rise of Puritanism* (New York: Columbia University Press, 1938).

Hamīdeh, Abdul-Razzaq, *Shayatinush-Shir'er* (*Poetic Devils*) (Cairo: Anglo-Egyptian Library, 1956).

Hamilton, G. Rostrevor, *Hero or Fool? A Study of Milton's Satan* (London: G. Allen Unwin, 1944).

Hanford, James Holly, *A Milton Handbook* (New York: Appleton-Century-Crofts, 1946).

—— 'The Youth of Milton', rpt. in *John Milton: Poet and Humanist*, ed. John S. Diekhoff (Cleveland: Press of Case Western Reserve University, 1966), pp. 75–125.

—— 'Milton In Italy' in *Annuale Mediaevale* 5 (1964), pp. 49–63.

—— 'The Chronology of Milton's Private Studies' in *PMLA* 3 36 (1921), pp. 251–314.

Hartman, Geoffrey, 'Milton Counterplot' in *English Literary History* 15 (March 1958), pp. 1–12.

Hill, Christopher, *Milton and the English Revolution* (New York: Viking, 1978).

Hitti, Philip K., *Islam and the West: A Historical Cultural Survey* (Princeton: D. Van Nostrand Company, 1962).

—— (trans.) *Memoirs of Usamah Ibn Munqidh* (New York: Columbia University Press, 1929).

Holt, P.M., 'The Study of Arabic Historians in Seventeenth Century England: The Background and Work of Edward Pococke' in *Bulletin of the School of Oriental and African Studies* 19 No. 3 (1957), pp. 427–55.

Hughes, Merritt, *Ten Perspectives on Milton* (New Haven: Yale University Press, 1965).

Hussein, Ṭāhā, *Tajdid dhikra abial-Ala* (*Renewal of the Memory of Abu al-Ala*) (1914; rpt. Cairo: Dār Al-Ma'ārif, 1922).

Irving, Thomas B. (trans.), *Kalila and Dimnah* (Newark: Juan de la Cuesta, 1981).

—— *Islam and the Missions: Papers Read at the Second Missionary Conference on Behalf of the Mohammedan World at Lucknow*, 23–28 January 1911. ed. E.M. Wherry et al. (New York: F.H. Revell, 1911).

Jones, L. Bevan, *Christianity Explained to Muslims: A Manual for Christian Workers* (Calcutta: Y.M.C.A. Publishing House, 1938).

Kastor, Frank S., 'In his own Shape: The Stature of Satan in Paradise Lost' in *English Language Notes* 5 (1968), pp. 264–9.

Kelley, Maurice, *This Great Argument* (Princeton: Princeton University Press, 1941).

Kinross, Lord, *The Ottoman Centuries: The Rise and the Fall of the Turkish Empire* (New York: Morrow Quill Paperback, 1977).

Knight, G. Wilson, *The Burning Oracle: Studies in the Poetry of Action* (AMS, 1939).

Knott, John R. Jr., 'The Visit of Raphael: Paradise Lost V' in *Philological Quarterly* 47 (1968), pp. 36–42.

Kranidas, Thomas, 'Dalila's Role in Samson Agonistes' in *Studies in English Literature* 6 (1966), pp. 125–37.

Kritzeck, J., *Peter the Venerable and Islam* (Princeton: Princeton University Press, 1964).

Kurath, Burton, *Milton and Christian Heroism: Biblical Epic Themes and Forms in Seventeenth Century England* (Hamden: Archon Books, 1966).

Leavis, F.R., *The Common Pursuit* (London: Chatto and Windus, 1952).

Le Comte, Edward, *A Milton Dictionary* (New York, Philosophical Library, 1961).

Lerner, L.D., 'The Miltonic Simile' in *Essays in Criticism* 4 (1954), pp. 297–308.

Letts, M., *Sir John Mandeville, The Man and his Book* (London: 1949).

Lewalski, Barbara K., 'Samson Agonistes and the Tragedy of the Apocalypse' in *PMLA* 85 (1970), pp. 1050–62.

Lewis, Archibald R., *The Islamic World and the West* (London: John Wiley and Sons Inc., 1970).

—— *Poetics of the Holy: A Reading of Paradise Lost* (Chapel Hill: University of North Carolina Press, 1981).

Lewis, C.S., *A Preface to Paradise Lost* (London: Oxford University Press, 1942).

Low, Anthony, *The Blaze of Noon: A Reading of Samson Agonistes* (New York: Columbia University Press, 1974).

Lowes. J.L., *The Road to Xanadu: A Study in the Ways of the Imagination* (London: Constable and Company, 1927).

Maleyn, Muḥammad, *Asir al-Mansur al-Muwahidi* (*The Age of Al-Mansur the Mohad*) (The North African Printing Press, n.d.).

Martz, Louis, *Poet of Exile: A Study of Milton's Poetry* (New Haven: Yale University Press, 1980).

Marvell, Andrew, *Complete Poetry*, ed. George de F. Lord (New York: The Modern Library, 1968).

Matar, Nabil, *Europe Through Arab Eyes, 1578–1727* (New York: Columbia University Press, 2009).

Miller, Leo, *John Milton Among the Polygamophiles* (New York: Loewenthal Press, 1974).

Milton, John, *Complete Poetry and Major Prose*, ed. Merritt Hughes (21 vols., New York: The Odyssey Press, 1957).

—— *The Works of John Milton*, eds. Frank Allen Patterson et al. New York: Columbia University Press, 1931–8).

—— *The Poems of John Milton*, ed. Alistair Fowler and John Carey (London: Longman, 1963).

—— *The Complete Poetical Works of John Milton*, ed. Douglas Bush (Boston: Houghton Mifflin Company, 1965).

—— *Paradise Lost, Books XI–XIII*, ed. Michael Hollington (Cambridge: Cambridge University Press, 1967).

—— *Paradise Lost, Books XI and XII*, ed. A.W. Verity (Cambridge: Cambridge University Press, 1918).

—— *Complete Prose Works of John Milton*, eds. Don M. Wolfe et al. (8 vols., New Haven: Yale University Press, 1953).

Mitchell, T., 'Philistia' in *Archaeology and Old Testament Study*, ed. D.W. Thomas (Oxford: Oxford University Press, 1964), pp. 405–27.

Mohl, Ruth, *John Milton and his Commonplace Book* (New York: Frederick Ungar, 1969).

Monro, James T. (trans.), *Hispano-Arabic Poetry: A Student Anthology* (Berkeley: University of California Press, 1974).

—— 'Muwashshahat' in *Collected Studies in Honour of Americo Castro's Eightieth Year* (Oxford, 1965).

Morley, Griswold S., 'A Note on Arabic Poetry and European Poetry' in *Hispanic Review* 8 (1939), pp. 344–6.

Mullinger, James B., *The University of Cambridge* (Cambridge, 1884).

Nardo, Anna K., *Milton's Sonnets and the Ideal Community* (Lincoln: University Of Nebraska Press, 1979).

Nicolson, Marjorie, *John Milton: A Reader's Guide to his Poetry* (1963; rpt. New York: Farrar, Straus and Giroux, 1970).

Nicolson, R.A., 'Mysticism' in *The Legacy of Islam*, ed. Sir Thomas Arnold and Alfred Guillaume (Oxford: The Clarendon Press, 1931), pp. 210–38.

Nykl, A.R., *Hispano-Arabic Poetry and Its Relation with the Old Provencal Troubadours* (Baltimore: J.H. Furst, 1970).

O'Leary, De Lacy, *Arabic Thought and Its Place in History* (London, 1926).

Osgood, C.G., *The Classical Mythology of Milton's English Poems* (London, 1926).

Ovid's Metamorphoses. Trans. Frank J. Miller (London, 1916; rpt. Bookprint, 1964).

Parry, John Jay (trans.), *The Art of Courtly Love by Andreas Capellanus* (New York: Frederick Ungar, 1959).

Peter, John, *A Critique Of Paradise Lost* (New York: Columbia University Press, 1961).

Pevsner, Nikolaus, *Cambridgeshire: The Buildings of England* (Harmondsworth, 1970).

Pickthall, Marmaduke (trans.), 'Translator's Foreword' in *The Meaning of the Glorious Qur'an* (London, 1930; rpt. New York: Muslim World League, 1977).

Poole, Austin L., *From Domesday Book to Magna Carta 1087–1216* (2nd ed. Oxford: The Clarendon Press, 1964).

Potter, G.R., *The New Cambridge History,* vol. 1 (Cambridge: Cambridge University Press, 1964).

Purchas, Samuel, *Hakluytus Posthumus or Purchas His Pilgrimes* (20 vols., Glasgow, 1905–7).

Rajan, B., *Paradise Lost and the Seventeenth Century Reader* (London: Chatto and Windus, 1947).

Rescher, Nicholas, 'The Impact of Arabian Philosophy on the West' in *The Islamic Quarterly* 10 (Jan–June 1966), pp. 3–11.

Rice, A., *Crusaders of the Twentieth Century* (London: Church Missionary Society, 1910).

Riggs, G., *The Christian Poet in Paradise Lost* (Berkeley: University of California Press, 1972).

Robinson, F.N. (ed.), *The Complete Works of Geoffrey Chaucer* (Cambridge: Cambridge University Press, 1933).

Said, Edward, *Orientalism* (New York: Pantheon, 1978).

—— *Covering Islam: How the Media and the Experts Determine How we See the Rest of the World* (New York: Pantheon, 1981).

Said, Jamīl, *Az-Zahawi wa thawratuhu fil jahim* (*Az-zahawi and his Revolution in Hell*) (Cairo, 1968).

Sands, Donald B. (ed.), *Middle English Verse Romances* (New York: Holt Rinehart and Winston, 1966).

Sarton, G., *Introduction to the History of Science,* vol. 2 (Ballirnase, 1947).

Saurat, Denis, *Milton: Man and Thinker* (1944; rpt. London: J.M. Dent and Sons, 1964).

Schacht, Joseph, and Bosworth, C.E., *The Legacy of Islam* (Oxford: The Clarendon Press, 1974).

Semaan, Khalil (ed.), *Islam and the Medieval West: Aspects of Intercultural Relations* (Albany: State University of New York Press, 1980).

Shawcross, John T., *With Mortal Voice: The Creation of Paradise Lost* (Lexington: The University Press of Kentucky, 1982).

Shelley, P.B., 'A Defence of Poetry' in *The Oxford Anthology of English Literature*, vol. 2, eds. Frank Kermode and John Hollander (New York: Oxford University Press, 1973), p. 1073.

Sims, James H., *The Bible in Milton's Epics* (Gainesville: University of Florida Press, 1962).

Smith, Byron Porter, *Islam in English Literature*, eds. S.B. Bushrui and A. Melikian (New York: Caravan Books, 1977).

Southern, R.W., *Western Views of Islam in the Middle Ages* (Cambridge, Mass.: Harvard University Press, 1962).

Spitzer, Leo, *Classical and Christian Ideas of World Harmony* (Baltimore: Johns Hopkins Press, 1963).

Stein, Arnold, *Answerable Style: Essays on Paradise Lost* (Seattle: University of Washington Press, 1967).

Stern, S.M., 'Studies on Ibn Quzman' in *Andalus* 16 (1951), pp. 379–425.

Swaim, Kathleen M., 'Flower, Fruit, and Seed: A Reading of Paradise Lost' in *Milton Studies* 5, ed. J.D. Simmonds (Pittsburgh: University of Pittsburgh Press, 1973), pp. 155–76.

Tayler, Edward W., *Milton's Poetry: Its Development in Time* (Pittsburgh: Duquesne University Press, 1979).

Thompson, E.N.P., 'Milton's Knowledge of Geography' in *Studies In Philology* 16 (1919), pp. 148–71.

Thorpe, James, *John Milton: The Inner Life* (Huntington Library, 1983).

Tillyard, E.M.W., *Milton* (New York: Dial Press, 1930).

—— *The English Epic and Its Background* (New York: Oxford University Press, 1954).

—— *Studies in Milton* (London: Chatto and Windus, 1967).

Von Grunebaum, Gustave E., 'The Arab Contribution to Troubadour Poetry' in *Themes in Medieval Arabic Literature*, eds. Dunning S. Wilson and Speros Vryonis (London: Variorum Reprints, 1981), pp. 138–51.

Waldock, A.J., *Paradise Lost and Its Critics* (Cambridge: Cambridge University Press, 1947).

Warton, Thomas, *The History of English Poetry from the Twelfth to the Close of the Sixteenth Century*, vol. 1 (London, 1728).

Watt, M.M., *The Influence of Islam on Medieval Europe* (Edinburgh, 1972).

Whiting, George Wesley, *Milton's Literary Milieu* (Chapel Hill: University of North Carolina Press, 1939).

Wilkes, George A., *The Thesis of Paradise Lost* (Melbourne: Melbourne University Press, n.d.).

Wilson, A.N., *The Life of John Milton* (Oxford and New York: Oxford University Press, 1983).

Wittreich, Joseph (ed.), *The Romantics on Milton: Formal Essays and Critical Aides* (Cleveland: Press of Western Reserve University, 1970).

Notes

Chapter I

1 'Islamic learning' is here used to refer to the scientific and literary heritage produced by Muslims, regardless of their race or geographical location, in the Arabic language. 'Arabic scholarship' denotes a study of the linguistic medium in which that heritage is recorded.

2 Philip K. Hitti, *Islam and the West: A Historical Cultural Survey* (Princeton: D. Van Nostrand Company, 1962), p. 50.

3 Norman Daniel, *Islam and the West: The Making of an Image* (Edinburgh: Edinburgh University Press, 1980), p. 142.

4 'Translator's Foreword' in *The Meaning of the Glorious Qur'ān* (London, 1930; New York: Muslim World League, 1977).

5 Karl H. Dannenfeldt, 'The Renaissance Humanists and the Knowledge of Arabic' in *Studies in the Renaissance* 2 (1955), pp. 97, 98.

6 Ibid., pp. 9, 816.

7 For a survey of the references to this legend, see Samuel Chew, *The Crescent and the Rose: Islam and England during the Renaissance* (New York: Oxford University Press, 1937), pp. 412–22.

8 *The Works of John Milton*, ed. Frank A. Patterson et al. (New York: Columbia University Press, 1931–8), pp. 5, 169–70. Henceforth referred to as Columbia Ed.

9 *A Relation of a Journey Begun An. Dom. 1610.* 6th ed. (London, 1670).

10 Daniel, pp. 282–3.

11 *Memories of Usamah Ibn Munqidh*, tr. P.K. Hitti (New York: Columbia University Press, 1929), p. 161; *Ibin Khaldun's Al-Muqaddimah*, tr. F. Rosenthal (New York, 1958), I, 107 ff and 168 ff.

12 Donald B. Sands, ed., *Middle English Verse Romances* (New York: Holt, Rinehart and Winston, 1966), Introduction, p. 5.

13 Thomas B. Irving, tr., *Kalīla and Dimnah* (Newark: Juan de la Cuesta, 1981), Introduction, p. xi.

14   Gustave E. von Grunebaum, 'The Arab Contribution to Trobadour Poetry' in his *Themes in Medieval Arabic Literature*, ed. Dunning S. Wilson and Speros Vryonis Jr. (London: Variorum Reprints, 1981), p. 147.

15   H.T. Chaytor, *The Troubadours* (1912; rpt. Kennikat Press, 1970), p. 47.

16   M.M. Watt, *The Influence of Islam on Medieval Europe* (Edinburgh, 1972), p. 61.

17   Earlier studies of Islamic influences on Dante's *Divine Comedy* include E. Bloche, *Les Sources orientales de la Divine Comedie* (Paris, 1901) and. A. de Gubernatis, *Su Le orme de Dante* (Rome, 1901).

18   Nicolson, R.A., 'Mysticism' in *The Legacy of Islam*, ed. Sir Thomas Arnold and Alfred Guillaume (Oxford: The Clarendon Press, 1931), p. 228.

19   Karl H. Dannenfeldt, pp. 102–03.

20   W. Wilson Cash, 'The Contribution of Islam to the Making of Modern Europe', in *Christendom and Islam: Their Contacts and Cultures Down the Centuries* (New York and London: Harper and Brothers Publishers, 1937), p. 109.

21   Nicholas Rescher, 'The Impact of Arabic Philosophy on the West' in *The Islamic Quarterly*, 10 (January–June 1966), p. 11.

22   *Dictionary of National Biography* (hereafter *DNB*), 5, p. 22.

23   The manuscript is in the Bodleian library (Ms. e Mus, 200). See Dannenfeldt, p. 116 n. 121.

24   *DNB*, 2, pp. 119–23.

25   James Bass Mullinger, *The University of Cambridge from the Election of Buckingham to the Chancellorship in 1626 to the Decline of the Platonist Movement* (Cambridge: Cambridge University Press, 1911), p. 94.

26   Arthur J. Arberry, *Oriental Essays: Portraits of Seven Scholars* (New York: Macmillan, 1960), p. 21.

27   P.M. Holt, 'The Study of Arabic Historians in Seventeenth Century England: The Background and the Work of Edward Pococke', *Bulletin of the School of Oriental and African Studies* 19, 3 (1957), p. 544.

28   Daniel, p. 2.

Chapter II

29 *Endowments of the University of Cambridge*, ed. J.W. Clark (1904), pp. 173–4.

30 Harris Fletcher, *The Intellectual Development of John Milton* (Urbana: University of Illinois Press, 1961), p. 380.

31 David Masson, *The Life of John Milton* (Macmillan, 1859–94), I, p. 161.

32 Tr. John S. Diekhoff in *Milton on Himself: Milton's Utterances Upon Himself and His Works* (New York: Oxford University Press, 1939), p. 135.

33 Tr. Masson, I, pp. 633–4.

34 Quoted in *The Christian Doctrine in The Works of John Milton*, ed. Frank Allen Patterson et al. (New York: Columbia University Press, 1931–8), pp. 19, 215.

35 Quoted by Helen Darbishire, *The Early Lives of Milton* (1932; rpt. New York: Barnes and Noble, 1963), pp. 60–1.

36 John Milton, *Complete Poems and Major Prose*, ed. Merritt Y. Hughes (New York: The Odyssey Press, 1957), p. 639. Henceforth referred to as Hughes.

37 George H. Turnbull, *Hartlib, Dury and Comenius* (London: 1947), p. 156.

38 Edward Frye, 'John Seldon', *Table Talk of John Selden*, ed. Frederick Pollock (London, 1927), p. 171.

39 Ibid., 3, pp. 483ff.

40 Hughes, p. 727.

41 Louis Bredvold, 'Milton and Bodin's Heptaplomeres' in *Studies in Philology* 21 (1934), p. 399.

42 Hughes, p. 741.

43 'Prolusion 7', Hughes, p. 626.

Chapter III

44 Quoted by George Wesley Whiting, *Milton's Literary Milieu* (Chapel Hill: University of North Carolina Press, 1939), pp. 68–9, from *The History of Diodorus Siculus*, ed. H.C. Gent (London, 1933–5), pp. 141–2.

45 See Verity's edition of *Paradise Lost* (Cambridge: Cambridge University Press, 1910), pp. 455–6.

46 Robert Cawley, *Milton and the Literature of Travel* (Princeton: Princeton University Press, 1951), p. 72.

47 See Geoffrey Hartman, 'Milton Counterplot', *English Literary History* 15 (March 1958), pp. 1–12.

48 Helen Gardner, *A Reading of Paradise Lost* (Oxford: The Clarendon Press, 1965), p. 80.

49 G. Wilson Knight, *The Burning Oracle: Studies in the Poetry of Action* (AMS Press, 1939), p. 85.

50 Quoted by Whiting, p. 69.

51 See Albert R. Cirillo, 'Time, Light, and the Phoenix: The Design of Samson Agonistes', in *Calm of Mind: Tercentenary Essays on Paradise Regained and Samson Agonistes in Honor of John S. Diekhoff* (Cleveland and London, 1972), pp. 209–33.

52 Ovid, *Metamorphoses*, tr. Frank J. Miller (London, 1916; rpt. Bookprint Limited, 1964), 2, p. 393.

53 Edward Gibbon, *The Decline and Fall of the Roman Empire*, ed. Bury. 5, p. 334.

54 Hughes, pp. 28–9.

55 Cawley, p. 118.

56 Quoted by Whiting, p. 58.

57 'Bermudas', in *Andrew Marvell: Complete Poetry*, ed. George DeForest Lord (New York: The Modern Library, 1968), pp. 10–11.

58 Hughes, p. 232 n. 2.

59 See Chew, p. 219 n. 1.

60 John W. Draper, 'Milton's Ormuz', *Modern Language Review* 20 (1925), p. 27.

61 In making Dalila Samson's wife, not his mistress as is the case in the Old Testament, Milton sharpens the conflict between patriotism on the one hand and matrimonial obligations on the other. Dalila tells Samson outright that her national duties come first. Certain critics treat her as a temptress and traitress, and, consequently, compare her to Satan in *Paradise Lost* and *Paradise Regained*. See for example Thomas Kranidas, 'Dalila's role in Samson Agonistes', *Studies in English Literature* 6 (1966) pp. 125–37, and Barbara K. Lewalski, 'Samson Agonistes and the Tragedy of the Apocalypse', *PMLA* 85 (1970), pp. 1050–62. However, Dalila should also be viewed as a philistine patriot.

62 Quoted by Hughes, p. 590 n. 1634.

63 See Masson's edition of *Paradise Lost* (Books 11 and 12) (Cambridge: Cambridge University Press, 1918), p. 66.

64 *The Complete Prose Works of John Milton*, vol. 1 (Yale: Yale University Press, 1971), p. 457, n. 21.

65 Columbia Ed., 5, pp. 169–70. See also p. 282 for similar analogies.

66 Thuanus' *Historia* (Geneva, 1626).

67 See Commonplace Book in Columbia Ed., 18, p. 211.

68 Commonplace Book in Columbia Ed., 12, p. 271. See Daniel, p. 14.

69 Hughes, p. 745.

70 *The Dialogue Concerning Tyndale*, ed. W.E. Campbell (London, 1927), pp. 305–6.

71 *Of Reformation* (1641), Columbia Ed., pp. 3, 44.

72 Columbia Ed., 13, p. 525.

73 J.E. Hurowitz, *Diplomacy in the Near East and Middle East: A Documentary Record 1535–1914* (1956; rpt. Dan Van Nostrand Company, 1958), pp. 5–6.

74 Lord Kinross, *The Ottoman Centuries: The Rise and Fall of the Turkish Empire* (New York: Morrow Quill Paperbacks, 1977), p. 321.

75 Quoted by Nabil Matar in *Europe Through Arab Eyes, 1578–1727* (New York: Columbia University Press, 2009), p. 20.

76 Ibid., p. 14.

77 James Mather, *Pashas: Traders and Travellers in the Islamic World* (New Haven: Yale University Press, 2010), p. 95.

78 Translated from Arabic by Professor Nabil Matar, op. cit., pp. 144–7.

79 *Christians and Jews in the Ottoman Empire: The Functioning of a Plural Society*, ed. Benjamin Braude and Bernard Lewis, Vol. I, p. 17.

80 See *Complete Works of John Gower*, ed. G.C. Macaulay (Oxford, 1899–1902), vol. 2, p. 239. In his definition of holy war, Milton adds the word 'Turks' to Gower's 'Sarazin'.

81 See Columbia Ed., 3, p. 36.

82 Hughes, p. 761.

83 See 3rd ed. (Cambridge, 1647), p. 8.

84   First entry in the Commonplace Book.

85   Milton's possible sources about the Turkish Empire were:
(1) *The General Historie of the Turkes* by Richard Knolles (1603). This
book was so popular that four editions (1610, 1621, 1631, 1638) were issued.
(2) Sandys' account in his *A Relation of a Journey*.
(3) Andrew Moore's *Compendious History of the Turks* (1660).
On Milton's familiarity (or lack of familiarity) with any of these
works, see Cawley, pp. 128–9, and E.N.P. Thompson, 'Milton's
Knowledge of Geography' in *Studies in Philology* 16 (1919), pp.
148–71.

Chapter IV

86   Maḥmūd al-Khafīf, 'Milton' in *Ar-Risālah* (*The Message*), 25
February 1946, p. 512. In the transliteration of Arabic names
I follow *The Cataloging Rules of the American Association and the
Library of Congress* (Washington: Library of Congress, 1959), pp.
38–45.

87   *Ar-Risālah*, 1 July 1946, p. 973.

88   Lord Macaulay, *Essay on Milton*, ed. H.B. Coterill (London:
Macmillan, 1925), pp. 44–52.

89   *Ar-Risālah*, 30 September 1940, p. 1087.

90   *Ar-Risālah*, 25 October, 1 November, 8 November 1937, pp. 1741–3,
1784–6, 1824–6.

91   Ibid., 25 October 1937, p. 1742.

92   Ibid., 1 November 1937, p. 1825.

93   Ibid., p. 1826.

94   *Ar-Risālah*, 9 December 1946, p. 1312.

95   *Ath-Thaqāfah* (*Culture*), 27 April 1948, pp. 17–19.

96   Ibid.; 14, 21 November 1939, pp. 16–18.

97   *Ath-Thaqāfah*, 21 November 1939, p. 17.

98   'Al-adab al-Inglīzī adab alamī' ('English Literature is an
International Literature'), *Al-Hilal* (*The Crescent*), 1 December
1967, pp. 219–22.

99   Columbia Ed., 3, pp. 376, 482.

100   Ibid., 8, p. 133.

101 *Doctrine and Discipline of Divorce*, in Hughes, p. 697.

102 Marjorie Nicolson, *John Milton: A Reader's Guide to his Poetry* (1963; rpt. New York: Farrar, Straus and Giroux, 1970), p. 240.

103 *Hakīm al-Ma'arrah* (*The Sage of Al-Ma'arrah*) (1944; rpt. Beirut: Al-Kashshāf, 1948), p. 127.

104 May 1886, pp. 440–56.

105 *Ilyadhat Homar* (*Homer's Iliad*), tr. Suleyman al-Bustani (Beirut, 1904), intro., p. 3.

106 *Tarīkh al-ādab al-Arabiyyeh* (*History of Arabic Literatures*) (Cairo: Al-Hilal, 1902), 2, p. 226.

107 See his translation of Macaulay's *Essay on Milton* (Cairo: Al-Khuniji Library, 1946), intro., p. 1.

108 *Al-ghufrān* (Cairo: Dār Al-Mā'arif, 1954), p. 325.

109 *Al-arabi* (*The Arab*), September 1967, pp. 52–7.

110 Safā Khulūsī, *Dirāsāt fil adab al-muqāran wal madhahib aladd-abiyyeh* (*Studies in Comparative Literature and Literary Schools*) (Baghdad: Al-Rabitah, 1957), pp. 102–3.

111 Ibid., p. 102.

112 A.J. Waldock, *Paradise Lost and Its Critics* (Cambridge: Cambridge University Press, 1947), pp. 77–8.

113 Arnold Stein, *Answerable Style: Essays on Paradise Lost* (Seattle: University of Washington Press, 1967), p. 124.

114 Khulūsī, pp. 98–101.

115 *Ar-Risālah*, 25 November 1946, p. 1313.

116 John T. Shawcross, *With Mortal Voice: The Creation of Paradise Lost* (Lexington: The University Press of Kentucky, 1982), p. 33.

117 'A Defence of Poetry' in *The Oxford Anthology of English Literature*, ed. Frank Kermode and John Hollander (New York: Oxford University Press, 1973), 2, p. 753.

118 Hughes, p. 179.

119 Abas Mahmud al-Aqqād; *Iblīs* (Beirut: Dār al-Kitāb al-Arabi, 1969), p. 15.

120 See *Iblīs*, pp. 201–3.

121 See Abas Mahmud al-Aqqād; *Majmu'āt Al-amāl al-Kāmilah* (*Complete Works*) (Beirut, 1979), 12, p. 378.

122 *Iblīs*, p. 219.

123   Ibrahīm Abdul-Qadir Al-Mazinī, *Al-Shiʿar: ghayatuhū wa wasaʾluhu* (*Poetry: Its Functions and Medium*) (Cairo, 1915), p. 5.

124   Hamdī As-Sakūt, see 'Ash-Shaytān: Al-ʿAqqād and Milton', *Fusūl* (*Seasons*), July 1981, pp. 163–72.

125   Al-Aqqād, *Complete Works*, 2, p. 336.

126   See *Iblīs*, 219, pp. 221–2.

127   See Jamīl Saʾid, *Az-Zahawi wa thawrathu fil Jahīm* (*Az-Zahawi and his Revolution in Hell*) (Cairo: 1968), p. 9.

128   Ibid., p. 33.

129   Khulūsī, p. 95.

130   See *Az-Zahawī: dirāsāt wa nusūs* (*Az-Zahawī: Studies and Texts*), ed. Abdul-Hamid al Rashadi (Beirut, 1966), p. 456.

131   See *Al-Majeleh Al-Jadeedeh* (*The New Journal*), April 1936, vol. 4, p. 329.

132   'Min al-Firdaws al-Mafqud' 'From *Paradise Lost*,' *Ar-Risalah*, 10 January 1937, pp. 778–80.

133   *Al-firdaws al-mafqūd: Malhamet al-Shāʾir al-Inglīzī John Milton* (*Paradise Lost; The Epic of the English Poet John Milton*) tr. and with an introduction by Muḥammad Anānī (Cairo: Al-Hayeh al-Masri-yyeh alʾammeh lil-Kitāb, 1982).

134   *As-Siyasah al-Usbuʾiyyah* (*Weekly Politics*), 11 June 1930, p. 24.

135   Khulūsī, pp. 118–25; 157–8; 148–9.

136   Nicolson, *John Milton*, p. 92.

137   Khulūsī, p. 149.

Postscript

138   Karen Armstrong, *The Battle for God: Fundamentalism in Judaism, Christianity, and Islam* (London: Harper Perennial, 2004), pp. 154–5.

Index